CHRONICLE OF A SCOTCH-IRISH FAMILY

The Leslies of Abbeville, South Carolina
Volume I

To Franklin with
best wishes

Don Leslie

Donald W. Leslie

First Printing

Published by
Southern Lion Books
Historical Publications
1070 Jordan Road
Madison, GA 30650

www.southernlionbooks.com

Manufactured in the United States of America.

ISBN: 9781935272182

Library of Congress Control Number: 2013951898

The paper in this book meets the guidelines for permanence and durability of the Committee on Production Guidelines for Book Longevity of the Council on Library Resources.

INTRODUCTION

The past is not meant to be a hammock but a springboard. Anon.

This is a chronicle of a family of Scotch-Irish descent who were an integral part in the settlement and establishment of the small South Carolina community of Abbeville. They were not the first family to arrive in the area and were not to be the most famous nor of the highest social caliber, but their contributions are important and lasting.

The family to be chronicled in this narrative is one whose surname has been spelled in various ways, including Lesslie, Lessley, Lesly, Lesley and Leslie.

The South Carolina Leslies are descended from an illustrious Scottish family that have their beginnings in the 1000's A.D., producing many men of substance that were a part of historical events and contributed to the formation of that country.

Like so many Americans of Scottish ancestry, this family spent generations in Northern Ireland before arriving on the Colonial shores to help tame the wilderness and establish permanent settlements that bear their imprint to this day.

The earliest person that can be identified with a connection to the Abbeville Leslie branch is Thomas, who was born in 1725, and left Belfast in late August of 1765, and arrived in Charleston in late November of that year. He received a land grant of 400 acres that was surveyed in 1766 and recorded in January 1767. Unfortunately, that is the last bit of recorded information about him that has been found to date. He died April 17, 1778, and was buried in the grave yard that he and his brother John, started. It is now known as Upper Long Cane

Cemetery. His descendants did leave considerable information that will be a part of this chronicle.

With all our modern conveniences, it is hard to imagine an existence along the edge of a primeval wilderness among the perils of Indian attack, wild animal assault and just getting around in an alien world. The necessity of building shelter, clearing land and planting crops with nothing but basic tools such as axes, hoes, mattocks, hand saws, mallets and augers, add to the wonder of it all. The Leslie family, along with their neighbors, did however, carve out of this wilderness a well-defined community that includes churches, schools and infrastructure that is available for all to enjoy today. Hopefully the illumination of those events will create an awareness and interest in those ancestors involved in making it happen.

DEDICATION

The Leslie family of Abbeville has much to be thankful for as most, if not all, family members are aware. Not many families have a place that they can identify as an ancestral home that has an unseen perpetual welcome sign. It is unseen because it has never been necessary to display it except at reunions and then as a formality.

William Edwin and Annie Donnald Henry Leslie were married in 1893 and decided the farm William inherited could support a large family and set out to prove it. The number thirteen to some is considered unlucky but to Will and Annie it was the perfect number. Thirteen children by any standard is a large family. To have every one of those children turn out to be such beautiful, Christian, family oriented, loving people is a tribute to two people that had a dream and worked diligently to make it happen. The history of this family returning as often as possible to the home William and Annie created to renew their family connections is itself a tribute to them.

Creating a home and filling it with children is one thing, having that dream continue for 120 years is another. That welcome sign was not a figment of imagination all those years and one of the thirteen saw to it that it be made as permanent as possible. James (eleventh child) and his wife Martha made sure that no one ever arrived with less than a cordial reception nor left without realizing a sincere welcome. It also takes people to continue that cordiality and fortunately this family is blessed that James and Martha imbued their children with the same sense.

Jimmy and Steve have worked hard to help make that a reality. Since Franklin and Ann live at the farm part time, their efforts have been especially helpful for they have worked tirelessly to make sure the place is always in beautiful condition and that every visitor feels that old time welcome when they arrive.

A family wide thanks to the James Leslie family for their efforts.

TABLE OF CONTENTS

CHRONICLE OF A
SCOTCH-IRISH FAMILY

The Leslies of Abbeville, South Carolina
Volume I

Chapter One

THE BEGINNING: THE LESLIES OF ABBEVILLE, SOUTH CAROLINA

Webster's unabridged dictionary describes a chronicle as something that records or recounts history. Others relate that it is a history, a story or a narrative. For the following pages, all of the preceding will apply, for the recorder of the events is an unskilled writer who is unfamiliar with where one of these appellations ends, and another starts, or *if* there is any true difference between them.

Genealogy has become a thriving hobby and sometimes a business in the last part of the twentieth century and, so far, the twenty-first has seen no decline in its popularity. This work will employ aspects of the genealogy meme (a unit of cultural transmission), it will not be a genealogy study, but a record of an evolving family, their contributions to society and to each other, and, where possible, a pictorial history of its growth.

For most, defining the true beginning of their family has proved very difficult if not impossible. Not so with the family that is to be chronicled in this work. The Leslies know exactly when, where and the circumstances that contributed to the founding of their lineage. Picking names and dates of such important events without some background that describes the 'why', 'how' and 'when' seems a little self-defeating, so the following will, hopefully, help to avert the questions and doubts that normally accompany such claims.

The surname Leslie first appeared in northeastern Scotland around the 1200's, but the family it applied to was of older origins. The use of surnames began in the late 1100's and until that time, people were known by various means such as a given name in conjunction with a father's name such as Angus, son of John (in Celtic areas that would be Angus MacJohn) or a location, occupation or physical trait (John the Red). The first recording of Leslie was Lesslyn and then became deLesslyn. The famous Declaration of Arbrouth of 1320 records the Leslie signature as deLesley. When the Abbeville ancestors, Thomas and John, arrived in Charleston in 1765, Colonial Council Meeting minutes recorded their names as Lesslie. Shortly after arriving in what is now the Abbeville district of South Carolina it was changed to Lesly. In the late 1800's some families changed to Lesley while others to Leslie. This writer's father was born as Lesly but his father changed to Leslie in the early 1900's.

Though the Leslie name had its origin in Scotland, the following narrative will show that events in England and Hungary were locales that contributed to its beginning. Unlike Scotland, England had an early history of invasion and conquest, first by the Romans who stayed for almost 400 years, and, when they left, the Germanic tribes of Angles, Jutes and Saxons invaded and took virtually total control of the indigenous British tribes. That complete control continued until the Vikings began their assaults in the 900's and by the 1000's had gained control of a large part of the island.

Edmund II was the British king in the early 1000's, but was forced to give up part of his realm to Canute, a Danish Viking. After attempts to eliminate Edward, his oldest son and heir, King Edmund sent him to the Kingdom of Hungary to be beyond the reach of those wishing to end his dynasty. That action would lead his son to be known as Edward the Exile. Edmund died around 1016 and his brother, also named Edward, to be known as the Confessor, assumed the throne.

As an English prince, living within the royal Hungarian court, Edward would naturally be an ideal marriage prospect for the king's daughter. Edward did marry Agatha, daughter of King Stephan of Hungary. Their marriage produced three children - Edgar, to be known as the Atheling, (Saxon for heir), Margaret, and Cristina. In 1055 King Edward, the Confessor became ill so his nephew decided to return to England to be available to claim his place as king. With an entourage of his

2

wife, three children and a large group of Hungarians as servants, Edward traveled across Europe to reach England in 1057. Unfortunately, the Exile died shortly after arriving in his homeland and his uncle, the Confessor lived until 1066. Edgar, as the legitimate heir, expected to be named the new king, but William, Duke of Normandy, intervened by defeating the English army and claimed the English throne for himself. Though Edgar lived in the court environment for nine years, his foreign existence left him with little opportunity to form alliances and attract followers, and William the Conqueror and his Norman followers exerted such total control, there was little chance of defeating them.

With few other options, Edgar decided to return to Hungary and chartered a ship for the Saxon/Hungarian group to sail for France as the first step of their long journey back to the only home he knew. The English Channel has a history of violent storms and one of them blew the chartered ship north. The ship's master, seeking shelter, steered into the Firth of Forth and came to rest on the north shore near Dunfermline and the Scottish royal court. King Malcolm III, Canmore welcomed the shipwrecked victims and because of the condition of the ship, made provision for a lengthy stay.

That shipwreck set in motion events that would have historical significance, one of which involved the future founders of the family of Leslie. The most historically important event, though, was the marriage of King Malcolm and Edgar's sister, Margaret. This marriage produced several sons who succeeded their father as Kings, but, more remarkable, Margaret was later canonized and is now a revered Saint of Scotland.

Edgar's entourage of mother and two sisters retained their Hungarian servants, and among each group of servants was a Chamberlain who seems to have been a person that took charge of their patron's affairs and acted as a body guard when needed. The name of Bartholomew, Chamberlain to Margaret, is the only name to survive of the group. Margaret evidently chose wisely in selecting such a servant, for records indicate he was a young man of noble birth and well-endowed physically and intellectually. King Malcolm thought enough of him to put him in charge of Edinburg castle and Bartholomew was allowed to marry the King's sister, Beatrix. The union that took place in 1070 is recognized by the Lord Lyon, King of Arms (Scotland's authority on genealogy) as the foundation of the family of Leslie. Evidently Bartholomew was also knighted, for he is known to have selected a heraldic icon and motto that would have been required for that important position. Both the icon and motto are recorded as connected to an episode involving Bartholomew and Margaret with him acting in his capacity as her Chamberlain. While touring the country on horseback, they came to a burn (creek) in a state of flood. For her safety, he suggested that she ride with him and grip his belt when crossing the flooded burn. When she questioned whether the buckle of his belt would hold, he replied to just 'GRIP FAST'. That story was repeated in court on their return, and the buckle became the icon worn on the knight's shield.

As a wedding gift, King Malcolm awarded Bartholomew and Beatrix  land in several locations along the east coast of the country, the northern most being about 25 miles west of the present city of Aberdeen. The couple selected that location to make their home and erected a structure, common at that time, called a 'mot and bailey'. This consisted of a wooden tower, usually on an artificial hill surrounded by a wall of pilings, and a moat surrounding the piling wall. About two centuries later, a descendant of Bartholomew erected a stone castle at the same location. Over the years, that castle was abandoned and allowed to deteriorate until the late twentieth century when David Leslie, an Aberdeen architect, became so interested in his ancestral history that he purchased the ruin and the surrounding acres and rebuilt it.

The top photo is Leslie Castle as it appeared when David Leslie purchased the ruin. He reconstructed the building according to the original design with the exception of a modern heating system. Though the stone walls are several feet thick, a protective outside coating of a special stucco material is necessary because of the fierce winter weather. This castle is known as a tower house and is common for the period of its original construction.

The family grew in numbers and importance for soon sons married and created their own estates while others married heiresses who held title to property and titles of nobility which passed to the male. Several generations elapsed and found Leslies in the northwest along the Spey River and southeast to the province of Fife, producing many men of substance such as Barons, Earls, Dukes, Generals, Bishops and Diplomats.

The conquest of Briton by William of Normandy not only played a part in the origination of the family of Leslie, but also had many far reaching effects that were felt throughout the island. The introduction of the European style feudal system changed the nature of land ownership and wealth distribution in England and was later adopted by the Scottish royalty. Under this system, all land belongs to the King who then awards the land as estates to loyal supporters, usually a Knight, Lord, Baron, Earl or Duke who agree to provide armed and trained fighting men when called upon by the king. This system also includes a provision of primogeniture which mandates that the oldest son inherit the father's estate and any titles of nobility that may be involved. This resulted in retaining the large estates that could better support the king with trained soldiers. This also resulted in younger sons with few options about their futures but to seek ways of establishing their own estates or careers. Many heads of families owning estates did buy lands outside of their primary properties and bequeath them to younger sons that usually resulted in the creation of *cadet* families, (younger sons that created estates and became known by that estate name, i.e. John Leslie of Kincraigie). As an example, the 4th Baron of Balquhain bequeathed one son with the title of Baron and the Balquhain estate, and three other sons with lands purchased or obtained by grants that resulted in three new estates – Kincraigie, Wardis, and New Leslie, and from New Leslie two more estates were created – Kinevie and Drummuir. The Laird of Drummuir had six sons, and it appears that five of them received no inheritance, but were required to seek their own way.

Careers were few and restricted to serving in the military, entering the church to become a priest, or becoming a farmer as a small land holder. The military ranks are full of Leslies in the 1600's and later, but before that there was no standing army so permanent military positions were almost nonexistent with the exception of becoming a knight, and that required a significant investment.

Enter the 1600's and tumultuous times for all Scots, but for the small land holders and even cadet families, it became devastating times. This one century saw the religious conflicts between the British government forces and the Scottish Presbyterians that included two wars, religious persecution that produced a period known as the 'killing times', the Darian scheme that saw a large proportion of the nation's capital wealth dissipated in a failed project, and a several-year drought that caused large numbers of Scots to immigrate to Northern Ireland.

SCOTLAND

Scotland is a country about the size of the state of South Carolina and a population that was small in relation to its size. For 900 years it existed as a free and independent nation, and then in the 1700's joined with England in a union that created Great Britain. In his "History of Scotland", J.D. Mackie stated "the act of union was a remarkable achievement. It made two countries one, but deliberately preserving the church, the Law and the Judicial system and some of the characteristics of the smaller kingdom, it ensured that Scotland preserve the definite nationality which she won for herself and preserved so long."[1]

Scottish character has surfaced in many ways, establishing an identity over the years which would recognize the Scots as unique among the world's peoples. Foremost of these traits was becoming the most literate country in the world due to the Presbyterian insistence of establishing schools in conjunction with each Kirk (church). This educational principle was first inspired to insure the ability to read and understand the Bible. It was soon realized that the process of learning was unusually compatible to the Scottish mind, so the concept was broadened to a national institution when local officials began assuming the responsibility of providing facilities and teachers. This happened long before literacy for the working class/laborers was considered to be important. As Lord Macaulay in his history of England most succinctly described the Scot, "to whatever land the Scotchman might wander, to whatever calling he might betake himself, in America or India, in trade or in war, the advantage which he derived from his early training raised him above his competition. If he was taken into a warehouse as a porter, he soon became a foreman. If he enlisted in the Army, he soon became a serjent."[2]

---

[1] A History of Scotland by J.D. Mackie, page 263
[2] The History of England by Lord Thomas Babbington Macaulay, Vol. IV page 302

Another national characteristic of the Scots is their devotion to the idea of family which springs from the CLAN concept. In Celtic, 'Clan' means family, and that has been, and continues to be, a powerful force among them no matter where they find themselves. Appreciating one's family is not a novel idea, but the Scots take the notion to a higher level than most, celebrating at gatherings, festivals and Scottish games throughout the world, proudly displaying their family tartans, sharing memorabilia, and strengthening family connections. Scottish games usually close with a ceremony that brings the Pipe and Drum bands (usually several) to a reviewing stand to 'pipe in' the different Clans separated by their own banners and stand before the reviewing councils as proud descendants of Scotland – a perfect place to savor the sound of the BAGPIPES.

When thinking of Scotland and national character, one must consider the fierce independent spirit the Scots have displayed for centuries. That spirit has fostered a 'can do' attitude that has propelled them to leading positions all over the world in every profession and trade. Though strong in many ways, Scotland has never had the industrial capacity or the agricultural potential that was prevalent in other European countries. England was a powerful military force, resulting from the Norman influence, that annexed Wales, an independent country. For two centuries the Normans tried to annex Scotland as well. The resulting invasions left Scotland with devastation and depleted resources – material, population and agricultural, but not in resolve. England won many battles but not the war.

In the era of the 1400's to 1700's, the country lived on the edge and little setbacks had profound effects. In an effort to improve their foreign trading potential in the late 1600's, a scheme known as the Darian project was devised to establish a foreign colony. The area that was selected for this colony was the Isthmus of Panama, for no other country had visible interest there. That effort was so popular among the people, and especially the nobility, that it attracted monetary subscriptions to support it which amounted to almost a third of the capital wealth of the entire country. When it failed because of poor planning, terrible local conditions (conditions faced by the French that prompted them to abandon the canal project and later Americans who finished it), English obstructions and Spanish opposition, Scotland was devastated. Unfortunately, that was not the only problem the country was faced with at the time. Nature was working against the country as well by inflicting a nationwide drought that crippled the small farming community so severely that families were forced to abandon what generations had toiled to perfect. Later the effects spread to the general population. King James VI was very aware of the problems that beset the country but was powerless to adopt measures that could alleviate the suffering as the resources the country processed were inadequate to meet the need.

Queen Elizabeth I of England died in 1603, unmarried, and thus without an heir. This led to a search for a successor to the throne. James VI of Scotland, the son of Mary, Queen of Scots was deemed the closest kin to Elizabeth and was selected to be the new ruler. He assumed the throne as James I and brought with him many ideas that have had long range effects.

The border between England and Scotland was an area that experienced almost constant guerrilla warfare for centuries with one side raiding the other, destroying property, stealing cattle and causing havoc, and the other side reciprocating. Both England and Scotland had vocally denounced the practice but looked the other way politically. When King James VI of Scotland became James I, he was King of both countries and the border conflicts became one of the first things he sought a solution to.

Another thorny issue that bedeviled England was the Irish problem. England invaded Ireland in the 1100's, and for 500 years endeavored to control the Irish population with only limited success. Though the whole island resisted the English, the most troublesome region was the province of Ulster, the most northern of the country, and the closest to Scotland. By various methods, some bordering on brutal, England gained control of large areas of the land in Ulster. James I was very practical and clever and he used those attributes to solve both the border problem and the Ulster situation, and the long range result had a very significant effect in assistance in solving a third. The English/Scottish border hostilities were quelled and remain so, but brought about a conflict that still rages in Ulster, an area we know today as Northern Ireland.

"ULSTER PLANTATION" – NORTHERN IRELAND

The solution to both the border and Ulster problems was the creation of the Ulster Plantation. Normally a plantation, as we know the term, is a large-acre farm in the southern United States, but in Ulster it covered the nine-county province, almost a quarter of the island of Ireland, though not all the land in those counties was a part, just areas within each county.

The creation of the plantation involved the confiscation of property that belonged to the Earls of Tyrone and Tyrconnell. When they revolted against the English government and were defeated, the Earls fled the island. England then used the attributes of the feudal system to claim their land as a reversion to the King. English and Scottish protestant settlers were then introduced to manage the confiscated land. Most of the Scottish settlers were from the border regions and their absence from the borders reduced the population to the extent that tensions were decreased and peace more easily established. These lowland Scots were known for their dour personalities, quick tempers, willingness and ability to fight for their strong Presbyterian beliefs. They took those personalities to a land whose people were totally and vehemently Roman Catholic, committed to land that had been a part of their families for hundreds of years, and culturally so Celtic in their heritage, that there was little or no room for accommodation with the newcomers. The result was guerilla warfare much like the Scots had lived with all their lives. They were extremely adept at defending themselves, and generations later when their descendants came to the frontiers of America, they made excellent Indian fighters. The entire Irish population was not displaced, but the volume of English and Scottish settlers tended to make the province amenable to English control, and that satisfied the desires of James I and his government – solving two problems with one stroke and, to some extent, a third.

When the multiple problems of the late 1600's flared up in Scotland, the Ulster Plantation served as a convenient escape avenue for many destitute Scots. The method of land distribution in the original 1610 plan was to award tracts of land to English and Scottish nobles and they, in turn, leased their land to managers who actually dealt with the individual settlers by granting long term leases. When the leases expired, new lease agreements included higher fees for the same plots a settler had worked to improve for thirty or more years. Some would not agree to the new contracts and opted for other areas, leaving their farms for newly arriving Scots. While the original Scottish influx into Ulster was from the border regions, this late 1600 influx saw Scots from all sections of Scotland taking advantage of a situation that saved the lives of many. This is the period when most Leslies entered Northern Ireland.

Chapter Two

THE IRISH SOJOURN

The Ulster Plantation proved to be a resounding success as a solution for the various English problems but another area of success is generally over looked. The agricultural production achieved by the newcomers was of such proportions that it astounded the locals who had used the tools and routines of centuries past. New methods of land management and diligent attention by the new tenants produced spectacular results, encouraging more and more innovations. For English farmers it was probably not so different from the results they had realized back home, but the Scots were not accustomed to rich soil, and realized harvests unknown to them in their hardscrabble borders area. Soon more and more Scots from the lowlands and west coastal areas crossed the 13 to 15 mile seas to claim a share of the bonanza. When the Plantation began, the proportion between English and Scottish was about the same, but the English settlers were not as accustomed to the hardships as were the Scots, so after a few years that proportion swung decidedly in their favor. Then, it has been said, the whole Northern Province took on a Scottish atmosphere.

The native Irish rebelled against the English government in the 1640's and, after a prolonged struggle, were defeated, leaving much devastation. Many of the properties formerly occupied by Scots were left vacant either because those tenants were causalities of the rebellion, or were driven away by the chaos. When the traumatic times of the 1690's hit Scotland, the Ulster Plantation presented a perfect solution to those seeking an answer other than hunkering down and hoping for the best. The English or Scottish estate owners were eager to see their lands once again in productive use, and offered very good terms to entice new lessees. The lowlands and coastal areas had been drained of most of their excess population so these new conditions in Ulster offered opportunities for Protestants from areas of Scotland that had been essentially excluded in the past from participation in the Ulster experiment. The northeast and eastern areas of Scotland normally possessed the best farmland in the country so that is where the long drought had its most severe effect. Coincidently, these were the areas where almost all Leslies lived at the time, so, naturally, Leslie families from different sections took advantage of the opportunities offered in Ulster. It seems most of the Leslies landed in the eastern portion of Ulster that is comprised of counties Antrim and Down, but various lists of church records, hearth rolls (taxable assets), and court records indicate a smattering throughout the nine Counties that originally comprised that province. When the new immigrants arrived, religious toleration was practiced, agriculture was thriving, and productive land was available. Conditions in the province remained advantageous to the Scottish immigrants for years until landowners and/or their agents in charge of managing the estates began increasing rental rates beyond the ability for most to pay. Many were forced to relinquish properties that had been held on the long term leases. This "rack-renting" led to the first of the Ulster Scots' departures for America, and when the religious climate changed drastically, more decided to leave. Then British business interests managed to have laws passed that curtailed the wool industries to the extent that profits evaporated and the Scottish wellbeing soon became very tenuous.

The change in the business climate was soon followed by a change in the religious. The Scottish tenants were almost totally Presbyterian by faith, and usually very committed to the Calvinist ideals, while the English farmers were normally members of the Church of Ireland, a branch of the Episcopal Church of England. When the new Scots arrived, it appeared that no difference existed between the two sects, but soon there were demands of oaths declaring allegiance to the Episcopal principles. The Church of Ireland was deemed to be the national faith, and any other religion was considered to be in conflict, and that carried certain penalties adding to other frustrations affecting the Scottish inhabitants. Numerous Scots had originally emigrated from Scotland to Northern Ireland because of many of the same difficulties facing them now, and the possibility of making another move was being presented to them – a move that was similar to the one their ancestors made, but over much greater distances, with many more unknowns, and this move was to have vastly different consequences.

When the list of difficulties multiplied to an intolerable level, more and more people began listening with keen interest to the agents employed by the shipping companies. These agents were responsible for providing cargo for the ships owned by individuals, as well as those owned by companies whose fleets may include many vessels. The emigration movement began in the early part of the 1700's, and those wishing to test the stories about the bountiful fruits of the American Colonies had to charter ships to accommodate their numbers. As the number wishing to leave increased, ship owners realized a potential for profits by filling their vessels with human cargo. As these voyages became more successful, they began employing more agents to roam the country, touting the wonderful prospects that awaited them in America in an effort to fill their cargo holds to capacity. The agents became more active as the various Colonies began offering inducements, principally in free land with delayed or no taxation for certain periods, as well as other fringe benefits such as free farming implements.

The push of individual, governmental and ecclesiastic policies that made life more and more difficult for the Ulster Scots, and the pull of the American colonies' need for labor and warm bodies to help settle the vast hinterlands, created an ideal climate for the coming monumental flood of emigration that would take place in the ensuing years. R.J. Dickson in his "Ulster Emigration to Colonial America 1718-1775", an exhaustive study of the phenomena of Scotch-Irish peopling of America, estimated that 250,000 Ulster Scots emigrated during this period. Some historians have estimated a larger figure than Dickson's, and some smaller, but the 250,000 seems an appropriate number and has been documented by more background data than others have attempted. The early emigrants were more attracted to Pennsylvania and New England and then to the Eastern Shore. Later their attention was shifted to the Southern Colonies of the Carolinas and Georgia, partly because they were less crowded, but also because those two areas realized the advantage of these stalwart settlers and made provisions which made their areas more attractive to potential immigrants.

Chapter Three

COMING TO AMERICA

Beginning in the early 1700's, those Scottish tenant farmers who felt the weight of the combination of difficulties most heavily, started abandoning their leases to take advantage of opportunities to go to the American colonies. In some instances, Presbyterian ministers not only joined their congregations, but also led the efforts to find the means of immigrating to America. Some were able to pay for their passage; others, who could not, were willing to sell their labor as indentured servants for short periods, with freedom at the expiration of the term. Unfortunately, many of these early voyages ended in disaster, and some, unable to withstand the rough seas, returned to Ireland. Though there were many early failures, enough successes occurred to get word back to Ulster of the wonders of the unlimited opportunities existing in the colonies. Through the decades, immigration continued with some years showing large numbers and some with smaller, but the flow of disgruntled Scots populated the colonies on a continuous basis.

The French and Indian War, 1754-1763, slowed the influx into the colonies because most of the Scots tended to go to the frontier where land was most available, and, in many cases, totally free, whether intended to be that way or not. The Scots were notorious for claiming, settling and daring anyone to try to take the land from them – (squatting in today's vernacular). The frontier, of course, was the area of the most severe Indian attacks, which temporarily reduced the lure of cheap land in the eyes of the immigrants.

The war officially ended in 1763, but the dominant Indian tribe in the Carolinas was the Cherokee. That tribe ended its struggle in 1761, but they continued to raid isolated locations such as in the massacre of the Calhoun's at their Long Cane settlement just south of the site of the future village of Abbeville. After 1763, where there had been a constant wave of immigration, now it was more of a storm surge of people flooding the colonies. Part of this new surge was due to the end of the war, but a significant element was the realization by the Colonial authorities that there was a need for more protection of the settled coastal areas that a more populous back country would provide. There were also needs of revenue that could be gained by future taxation and trading opportunities with a populated countryside. There were other considerations as well, but the above tended to yield action that hastened an unprecedented growth of new Americans. In order to promote more immigration, the South Carolina Colonial Council began authorizing large tracts of land to be set aside called Townships for Protestant immigrants, some of which were intended for specific nationalities such as Boonesborough Township, where the survey states - "...laid out for the use of such foreign Protestants from the kingdom of Ireland as may arrive in the Province...", others such as Hillsborough for the French Huguenots, Saxe-Gotha for Germans, Purrysburg for Swiss, and there was even an area known as the Welsh Tract. This writer is not aware of the terms for other Townships, but it is known that Boonesborough offered 100 acres for the head of household and fifty acres for each additional family member given as a bounty at no cost to the new settler and no taxes for several years. In addition to the free land, farming implements were supplied to help clear the land of undergrowth and trees required to start cultivation.

A sailing ship known as a brigantine named The Prince of Wales was moored to a wharf in Belfast harbor in October, 1765, when two Lesslie brothers and their families came aboard with small parcels of belongings, hoping for good weather for a voyage that was expected to last two to three months. The ship was only 40 to 50 feet long and 25 to 30 feet wide, small by seagoing standards, but evidently well made. The cargo hold had been cleared of all normal cargo-securing devices and replaced by wooden shelves on both sides of the hold attached to the hull, and ran about six feet toward the center where they were secured by stanchions every four to five feet, and were stacked from floor (deck) to the deck above, spaced about two feet apart. To see what this arrangement looked like you need only go to the city of Omagh, Northern Ireland where there is an immigrant museum with an actual ship on display showing the type of accommodations travelers leaving Northern Ireland in this period would have experienced. The sleeping arrangements were not designed for comfort, obviously, but to accommodate the maximum number of passengers.

Most of the adults on this voyage were middle aged with children ranging from infants to teens. With little privacy for anyone, the close quarters over such a long period of time must have been extremely difficult. Preparation of meals, concern for hygiene and sanitation had to be carried out within the space between the shelving of the cargo hold, with few opportunities to visit the open deck above because of weather and lack of safety provisions. The one thing that made these conditions bearable was that they were accustomed to harsh living conditions. Of course, the sea and wave action must have been awful on such a small ship. This writer crossed the North Atlantic on an Aircraft Carrier in November accompanied by two other ships. The weather was so rough the two other ships were forced to return to the states with damage. Hopefully, the Prince of Wales left Belfast before the roughest weather set in. Regardless of the weather, it had to be a relief when Charleston harbor was sighted.

Thomas and John Lesslie had been enticed to use the Prince of Wales by agents of the ship's owners who were employed to travel around the areas deemed most probable of producing people interested in emigrating. These agents usually worked in pairs, with one in Ireland to record the passengers, and the other on the opposite end in America to collect any unpaid fees, or to arrange for employment for the indentured passengers. Fees were charged to each traveler helping cover the expenses of crossing the Atlantic to pick up normal trade goods produced by the American colonies such as lumber, tobacco, animal skins, and flax seed to be sold in Europe. The fees were evidently very small because most colonies also reimbursed the ships' owners for each immigrant delivered to their docks.

The Lesslies joined other families that had already come aboard and would wait until others joined to make the list of those expected complete so they could sail. Their destination was the American Colony of South Carolina where there were conditions that promised a new life.

The most important was the possibility of land they could actually own just as the great lords of their country did. The two families were part of a group with similar ambitions, hopes and dreams and shared common experiences and frustrations. They were Irish by birth but Scottish by culture, tradition and heritage. Their ancestors had left Scotland looking for the opportunity of a more productive life that would offer greater rewards for their labor and provide a better future for themselves and family. Now they were doing the same thing by leaving Ireland, but this move would prove to be a permanent solution with unimaginable results whose benefits would be felt over two centuries later with the promise of continuing into the future.

Upon reaching Charleston, the passengers of the Prince of Wales made application for the land that had been promised, and prepared to present themselves before the Colonial Council at the next available meeting date, occurring on December 4, 1765.

At this meeting the Council determined who had paid their passage fees, and those that did so were eligible for the promised bounty land. Each passenger was also examined as to whether certificates of good standing in their protestant affiliation were available. Both brothers qualified for the bounty, and each was awarded 400 acres, with both tracts located in Boonesborough Township. At least that is what the Council stipulated, however, the surveys state that the land is 'near Boonesborough' Township and has recently been determined by computer-generated location programs to be close to the town of Abbeville which lies several miles south of the area of the township. Thomas Lesslie, his wife Jane, both aged 40, and their children William 11, Margaret 8, Thomas 5, Jane 2 and evidently a sister of Thomas named Anne 30, and John Lesslie, his wife Mary, both aged 38, and their children William 13, Jane 11, Samuel 7, John 4, made their way to the northwestern area of South Carolina when all the requirements of the colony were satisfied. Since most of the other bounty recipients had received their lands in the Boonesborough area, it seems to be a safe assumption that they traveled as a group for safety and for the benefit of pooling their resources to provide transport provisions such as horses, wagons and other necessary equipment.

From Charleston to the Abbeville area is almost 200 miles, and it is beautiful country even today. What a wonder it must have been to the new arrivals to see all the undeveloped, forested land as they made their way north to their destination! The weather in December can be rather harsh at times, even in the Deep South, so it probably took the group at least three to four weeks to make their way over what was known as the Keowee Trail. The trail had been produced by the Indian traders making their way to the Indian Nations with trade goods, and then returning with animal skins, the primary product obtained from the trading operation to the coastal areas. The trail wound its way from Charleston to the north, crossing the Congaree River close to the present city of Columbia, and then past the trading post of Ninety-Six where the new arrivals left the trail and headed west to the 'long canes' area, the place they would call home.

They arrived there in late December or early January to find a wilderness occupied by a few settlers in scattered locations, but no provisions for shelter or other amenities. Since they had not chosen the location of their grants, only temporary shelters could have been erected to provide some comfort from the winter weather, and both brothers had very young children, so the conditions could not have been very pleasant. Somehow they survived and prospered.

The Cherokee Indians had ceded the lands around what is now Abbeville County only a few years previously, and showed their displeasure at the loss by raiding isolated settlers with much loss of life and devastation in the way of burned buildings and ruined crops. As a consequence, the new settlers were not only required to perform all their own chores, for slave labor did not reach this area until much later, but also act as militia units for protection and offensive patrols intended to punish those responsible for the destruction. There are many stories in the histories of the early years of the area of groups of local farmers organized as pursuing militias that tracked the offending Indians and destroyed them to a man, other forays only partially successful.

The Long Cane Presbyterian Church, the only Abbeville County Presbyterian Church for many years, and one of only three in the upper part of the colony in its formative years, was in the forefront of the frontier struggle, and many times acted as a rallying point for the organizers of these retaliatory raids. The history of the church relates that as late as 1780, the preacher was known to lean his long rifle on the pulpit with his shot pouch and powder horn over his shoulder as he led the services in order to be sure he was ready for any emergency. Though the history did not include any mention of the congregation bringing their arms into the church, it is almost certain they did.

The many stirring novels of the Iroquois, Mohegan and Mohawk Indians, and other northern tribes and their interplay with the settlers in those areas, were duplicated on the Carolina frontier with all the horror, bravery and determination as depicted by authors such as James Fenimore Cooper. This was not a place for the timid or weak, man or woman. Even the children were required to be supportive of their families in every way possible. The taming of this frontier, the formation of productive farms, installation of infrastructure and creation of civilizing influences such as churches and schools is a story of Herculean effort by a people who were obviously strong and hardy when they arrived, and made even tougher and more self-reliant by their successful mastery of the elements.

John Logan in his "History of Upper Carolina" describes the scene as the new arrivals would have seen it. "That fertile section of the old Ninety-Six district, which was afterwards known as the Flat-Woods of Abbeville, presented to the view of hunters and pioneer settlers, the magnificent prospect of the hills and valleys of an extended tract of prairie country, waving under the rich growth of cane, from five to thirty feet in height."[3] Some obscure biographer of John C. Calhoun stated that his father, Patrick, while living in Virginia, was in a party of guides that accompanied a group of settlers down the Great Wagon Road to its terminus at the Waxhaws. While there, they heard about the lands around Long Cane Creek and decided to see them before returning. When they saw the land covered in canes as stated above, they realized this land would be easier to clear than the normal forest growth of virgin timber.

---

[3] History of Upper Carolina by John Logan

They returned to Virginia and collected their families for a move to the 'cane' lands. They arrived in the area in 1756 and, being among the first settlers, had their choice of locations to establish their community. An area south of the present town of Abbeville was selected for their community along a creek that would later bear their name. They did what all settlers learn to do that claim land along the frontier – built cabins for shelter and security, cleared land for planting, and began enjoying the fruits of their labor.

The few inhabitants that preceded the Lesslies and their fellow immigrants were scattered over a wide area using rough paths in lieu of roads that had yet to be developed and with few businesses where supplies could be purchased. Settlers on a frontier such as this quickly learn to be very self-sufficient, and must do what is necessary with what they have, or create what they need. This was the leading edge of the frontier that was constantly being pushed further and further into the wilderness. Though the neighbors were few and scattered and roads nonexistent, people did come together when needs arose, like raising roof beams and other difficult tasks that single individuals were incapable of performing. Difficult and strenuous as the physical exertion must have been, the land did get cleared of obstructive growths, crops planted, and cabins raised and occupied under less than ideal conditions. "Horse thieves, cattle rustlers, gunmen, all the riffraff of civilization swept the region with terror - in orgies of pillaging, arson and rape-against which the outraged settlers had no legal redress at all."[4]

Patrick Calhoun led a group of neighbors to Charleston in 1767 to seek Colonial assistance in establishing some type of legal authority for the region, as well as roads, schools and representation in Colonial government. Their request went unheeded, so in 1769, Patrick led another contingent of area settlers to the nearest voting center which was 23 miles from Charleston. With their long rifles, ballots were seized to vote Patrick into government, and his presence persuaded members to begin providing the needed Colonial authority and financial means to remedy the inequities that existed. As in any governmental venture, the solutions did not occur overnight, but at least they were begun.

---

[4] John C. Calhoun, American Portrait by Margaret L. Coit, page 4

Thomas and his brother, John, proceeded in their efforts to fulfill the requirements of their land grants by clearing enough land for an initial planting, as well as erecting living quarters of log construction. The abundance of forest growth in the area and its simplicity made this type of structure the only feasible kind of housing considered by the early settlers. The first house erected in the village of Abbeville, even years later, was a log cabin and remained on the town square into at least the 1820's because one of the rooms served as John C. Calhoun's first law office. The first house on the farm, started in 1773, was of log construction. It was replaced only in the late 1850's by a one story frame cottage-style house. It was expanded into a two story house in the 1890's that this writer knew until adulthood. One of the rooms of the original log structure continued to be used as a shop building which was allowed to deteriorate over the years, as its use was no longer needed. The two story house was burned to the ground in 1971 due to a faulty chimney.

In 1876 Reverend Robert Lathan, D.D., Associate Reform Presbyterian minister, teacher, school administrator, theological professor and writer, created a history of South Carolina that was published serially in the Yorkville Enquirer newspaper, and the installments were later collected and printed as a manuscript by his grandnephew, Dr. S. Robert Lathan, M.D. In installment XXXIV he quoted Robert Witherspoon, immigrant from County Down, Ireland, in describing their experiences as new settlers in the Williamsburg section of South Carolina in 1734. Mr. Witherspoon wrote an essay about the entire journey from Belfast harbor, landing in Charleston, traveling overland to the land they had been awarded, and ended by stating, "We had a great deal of trouble and hardships in our first settling, but the few inhabitants continued to stay in good health and strength. Yet we were oppressed with fears on diverse accounts, especially being massacred by the Indians, of being bit by snakes, of being torn by wild beasts or of being lost in the woods. Of this last calamity there were three instances."[5] Such were the sufferings endured by the early settlers all along the frontier and probably for several years until they became more accustomed to their new environment.

---

[5] History of South Carolina by Rev. Robert Lathan D.D., Installment XXXIV

On the voyage across the Atlantic the brothers, Thomas and John, in a discussion about their future in an unknown environment, realized one of their family members was likely to succumb to some disease, accident, or other unfortunate event. The chances of having their properties adjacent to one another being slim, they decided that at the first death in either family they would meet between their homes and establish a burying ground if none existed. The custom at the time was to bury family members on one's own property, so no common burial area was available.

What they established is now known as Long Cane Cemetery, and is situated almost exactly half way between their original land grants as located by computer-generated programs and across the road from Long Cane Presbyterian Church, the oldest Presbyterian Church in upper South Carolina.

The first grave is believed to be that of one of John's servants, and the second is that of John himself. A memorial monument placed at the site of the first burial by the Long Cane Cemetery Association, describes the first buried as a servant in the John Lesslie household who was killed in an accident while making lye soap. Unfortunately, the monument contains the wrong date of 1760 rather the correct date of 1766.

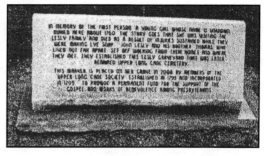

The grave sites of the two brothers are nearby, marked by simple

field stones with their initials and dates of death carved in the rough stone. At some later date, cement was placed around each stone and, even later, marble coping was added to set the two grave sites apart in a growing cemetery, shown on the left with several Leslie cousins during a 2011 celebration.

In 2010 a local group realized the historical significance of the cemetery and began compiling data necessary to obtain recognition by the state and federal governments. During 2011, the cemetery was placed on the Registry of Historic Places with an official placard placed there, and in a ceremony on November 27, 2011, it was officially recognized by local authorities as shown on the right.

This historic cemetery is the resting place of this writers parents, grandparents, one through four great-grandparents, six uncles, five aunts, great uncles and aunts, five cousins and two sons.

The new settlers had only ten years of relative peace to establish their farms into profitable operations when the Revolutionary War began. John Buchanan, in his historical depiction of the south, and more particularly South Carolina, in "The Road to Guilford Courthouse", relates the struggles of the people of this time. There were really two wars going on in the late 1770's to about 1781 or 1782. A great deal of the actual fighting was not only done in South Carolina, but also the crucial battles that decided the fate of the war were carried out in that state.

The battles of Cowpens and King's Mountain, both South Carolina sites, were American victories that convinced the patriots that the vaunted British army could be defeated. These victories were morale boosters that so changed the attitude of the young volunteers they no longer fled at the sight of the red-coated British regulars, but used their accurate long rifles with new found confidence. The state militias led by Andrew Pickens (from Abbeville), Thomas Sumter and Francis Marion, the Swamp Fox, proved to be a formidable force after they received some training.

The other war in the South was waged between those men who felt their loyalty was to England and the King (loyalists), and those who felt their loyalty belonged to the land that had provided them freedom such as they had never know (patriots), most of whom were Scotch-Irish, for there were many pacifist groups that refused to participate. The other way to delineate this second conflict is Tory (loyalist) against Whig (patriots). The first was a traditional one – set battles of one disciplined army against another (not quite as disciplined but at least organized) with clear results of one side winning, the other losing. Not so with the second war. This war was a vicious guerrilla, hit and run, civilian-oriented one with no intention of winning, but to intimidate by burning houses, barns and even churches, and murdering selected civilians. Many instances have been recorded of Tory raiding bands calling a man out of his house for a discussion and then brutally slashing him to death with their sabers in front of his wife and family. 'Bloody' Bill Cunningham was one of the more notorious of the Tory leaders, and another was Daniel McQuirk, or as young Thomas Lesly spelled it, 'McGirt'. Young Thomas claimed a Revolutionary War pension for his services in the war and was required to execute an affidavit detailing his war service. In that document he related that as a 19-year-old, he enlisted evidently as foot soldier, and then, a year later, served in a mounted militia unit under various commanders, including Gen. Andrew Pickens, Cols. Anderson, Clark and McCall. His unit was sent on one mission into Georgia along the Savannah River in search of Tories with orders to "take no Tory prisoners but if they found any that needed killing, not to spare them."[6] In the same document, he related that his unit rendezvoused on several occasions at his father's farm, and that there was no safety in the area unless under arms and their unit patrolling to protect against Tory raids, especially while the locals were harvesting their grain.

This was not an easy place to try to establish a farm, nor a safe one, but those tough minded Scotch-Irish not only hung in there and survived, but did it with gusto! These tough people with their strong backs, strong minds, strong spirits, and an indomitable determination to protect their freedom, just would not be denied. The sons and grandsons of Thomas and John, as well as a brother's son, all served in militia units and supplied food, tools and equipment during the war, being reimbursed in the later part of the 1780's for time served, as well as the provisions and gear.

---

[6] Affidavit by Thomas Lesly, son of Thomas

During this perilous time, Thomas managed to establish a farm on land that had been passed over by other settlers, probably because it contained high ground. Generally, cane growth did not occur on higher ground, and if it did support cane, it usually grew only a few feet high, indicating to these new settlers that the land was not as fertile as land supporting the higher growing cane, sometime reaching 20 feet or higher. This high ground also usually contained large trees, making that land harder to clear for agriculture. That farm, containing over 600 acres, is still known as Leslie Oaks. One of the redeeming factors of this land was that it was/is well watered, with creeks on both sides and a ridge down the middle, with many springs creating small creeks running to the side ones. It was evidently well managed since it became a profitable enterprise and continued to be such for 226 years, when small farming all over the country began to phase out. The actual working farm operation lasted a few years less, but the farm has continued to yield profits from timber sales and will, for the foreseeable future, from the pines planted in areas formally used as pasture, cotton and grain growing.

When slavery was discontinued in 1865, tenant farmers supplied most farm labor, essentially the same system and using the same housing, except now the former slaves worked on shares. The farm owner not only provided the housing but also small plots of land that were used as gardens that grew most of their vegetables, and received portions or shares of animals slaughtered on the farm such as hogs, cattle and sheep. Farm products such as wheat, oats and corn were distributed as flour, corn meal and processed oats on some type of pre-arranged basis. The sale of cotton usually provided the only cash the share cropper families received. Farm owners usually provided the necessary medical care and clothing, or cloth to make them. All the implements necessary to carry on a farming operation were owner-supplied, including horses, mules and oxen, plows, wagons, etc., and the seed and fertilizer. In return for the above, the tenant farmers provided the labor to produce the products that were <u>intended</u> to make the farm profitable.

During the Second World War, most of the tenant farming labor was diverted to factory employment, and after the war, government programs made farm labor (or almost any other type labor), unnecessary for survival. Farm owners also found it more profitable to find employment in towns around them, while trying to maintain some farming operations such as gardens, hay production and beef grazing – anything with little intensive labor requirement, but using available land and equipment. When that generation passed away, their children usually looked for more glamorous ways of earning a living, and the small farms became housing developments, or acres for wealthy individuals to use as tax write-offs, horse farms or cattle-raising. Fortunately for Leslie Oaks, the last owner, James Lewis Leslie* and his children were more interested in maintaining family ownership, and placed the remaining portion (after division between brothers) of over 275 acres in a trust that will probably not guarantee perpetual family possession, but certainly prolong it.

* James Lewis Leslie passed away in 2008, aged 95.

Before this narrative is continued, some misconceptions about the founding members of the Abbeville Leslies should be addressed. In the 1940's, members of the family commissioned Ms. Louise Reynolds to create a genealogy study of the family and, thanks to her; much of the extended family was recorded while many of the older members were still alive to add their knowledge of the ancestors they were aware of. Their memories, intense interest and abounding love of the Leslie family were of vital importance in preserving the knowledge we possess today of family that would have been lost without their timely input. Ms. Reynolds did a remarkable job of collecting the data and organizing it in a very readable form. It is very doubtful if this writer would have even considered an attempt to undertake this current version if it had not been for the information she supplied. Indeed, it was her study, as well as the many conversations by family members, that piqued the interest that has led to the further investigation helping to uncover information that changes some of her conclusions, and/or assumptions, and adds data in parts of the family that were omitted.

Ms. Reynolds identified William, Jr. as the founder of the family under discussion, for his life was confirmed by the existence of his will and other historical documents. The problem is the identity of his father. Ms. Reynolds states flatly that William, Sr. is the father of the person she identified as William, Jr., evidently assuming that since William used the sobriquet Junior, his father must also be named William. The only record of any kind to be found of another William in the area at the time was John's son, William, and a William, son of Samuel, another cousin.

Another item that apparently led to confusion about the father/son relationship was the Dec. 4, 1765, Colonial Council Meeting that recorded William, son of Thomas and Jane, as being 8 years of age, meaning that person's birth year would have been 1757, and his older sibling, 'Mark' as 11, but placed them out of order - 8 and then 11. Brent Holcomb published "Petitions for Land Grants from the SC Council Journals", and in Vol. 5 1757-1765, he shows the Dec. 4, 1765 entry of Jane Lesslie and children with Wm. as 8 with parenthesis next to it with notation of "variations in British copy." Fortunately, the British authority's people were more diligent in their record-keeping, and recorded the children of Thomas and Jane as William 11, and more clearly identify his sibling not as Mark, but as Margaret 8, (an attempt to abbreviate Margaret, and blurred ink, evidently made it look like Mart or Mark). William's age of eleven coincides with the family Bible information so should confirm that Thomas was William's father. Another error revealed by the British version shows the oldest sibling as Anne to be 30, and not 13, as the American version did. Anne was probably a sister of Thomas, for he was 40 at the time.

Other conditions exist that reinforce the relationship of Thomas and William. Thomas and his brother, John, were awarded 400 acres as their land bounty at the above mentioned meeting, and both grants were surveyed to be near Boonesborough Township the following year, but no record of a William with a land bounty has been found that year or any other year.

A second item that should help affirm the relationship is a system the Scots used in naming their children. This was not an absolute regimen, but was generally followed, and it became even more of a fixture with the Scotch-Irish. The system involved both male and female, but seems to have been followed more with males. The system required the first son to be named for his paternal grandfather, the second son for his maternal grandfather, and the third named for his own father or an uncle, etc. William's first son was named Thomas, who died very young, and a subsequent son was also named Thomas. John's son, William, named his first son John, and Samuel's son, William, named his first son Samuel.

A third reason to believe in the correct relationship is that genealogists who have studied the 18th century have stated that the term 'junior' was rarely, if ever, used then as it is today but to denote the younger of two boys with the same name. Consulting the written record of the Dec. 4, 1765 Colonial Council Meeting (see appendix), it shows John's son, William, to be 13, or two years older than the son of Thomas.

Another area of difference with the Reynolds' Manuscript is the method of arriving in the Abbeville area. She seemed to be unable to decide whether they came with many other settlers down the Great Wagon Road from Pennsylvania, or directly from Charleston. There seems little doubt that the Abbeville Lesslies arrived in Charleston by ship and made their way up the available trails to what was then Granville County, Ninety-Six District and the vicinity of Boonesborough Township.

There were Lesslies in the Waxhaw area, some of whom arrived there by way of that famous road, and others known to have traveled the paths from Charleston. Many of the Waxhaw family names are similar or identical to the Abbeville family, apparently causing much confusion, but comparisons of genealogy charts and last will and testaments of the two families show distinct differences. The two families were in their respective areas about the same time, and both profess County Antrim heritage, so it seems very likely that there were connections between the two back in Northern Ireland.

Another problem about the Reynolds' Manuscript is the omission of one of William's sons – that of John Harris as well as William's brother, Thomas. These branches should be included, if possible, since we are now really talking about the descendants of Thomas. Activities in Clan Leslie have brought information about these two families to the attention of this writer, and their stories will be included to the extent possible, hopefully making a truly complete family history.

One final item regarding the Reynolds' Manuscript needs to be addressed, that of the identification of William, son of Thomas as a junior. It appears from examination of all available sources that the only time William used that term was when he signed his receipt for Revolutionary War payment. The only reason for signing that way evidently was to differentiate between himself and his cousin, William, son of John. He never signed his surveys as Jr., and did not sign his last will as such.

His son, William, did however sign his name as Jr. on surveys. It must have been necessary to use Jr. because father and son were surveying at the same time and there was need for differentiation between related individuals. Both Williams' signed their names with very distinctive penmanship. A comparison of their signatures taken from various documents should confirm the identity of both, and establish the true relationship of father, son and grandson. Notice the three signatures of William, son of Thomas. The first as William, Jr. and the next two without the Jr., but the second on a survey as DS (Deputy Surveyor) he made in 1786, and the last one as a sixty-seven year old. The signature of William, son of William, is not as distinctive as his father's, but is still recognizable as the comparison below shows. The first signature is from his last will and testament, and the second is from a survey done in 1817.

From Militia Pay receipt	From survey of 1786	From last will and testament

Chapter Four

LESLIE OAKS, THE FARM

There is no record of Thomas Lesslie leaving a will, or of any other document, but we know that he and his wife, Jane, had only two sons, and his younger son, Thomas, left the Abbeville area soon after the Revolutionary War ended for Pendelton, S.C., and later moved to Tennessee.

The oldest son, William, did leave a will (see appendix), and in it he left his farm, consisting of 650 acres, not to his oldest son, but to a younger one named William. That William executed a will (see appendix) to his two surviving sons, Alpheus E. and John J. An agreement showing that John J. sold his half interest to his brother, Alpheus E., was recorded at the court house, and a copy is shown in the appendix. John J. moved to the nearby town of Anderson shortly after his father's death and began a farm close to the city. William remained on his father's farm and raised his family there. So far, a will by Alpheus E. leaving the farm to his only son, another William, has not been found, but it may yet turn up as the 'buy out' agreement recently did. While looking through some old papers, an insignificant-looking folded paper, when unfolded, revealed the agreement.

Alpheus's son, William Edwin, did leave a will stipulating that the farm be sold and the proceeds shared equally between his thirteen children. His wife, Annie Henry Leslie, added a provision that the field across the road, consisting of about 35 acres, be divided into thirteen lots, with each child, or their heirs, receiving a lot (all lots amounted to about 2 1/2 acres each).

At the death of Annie in 1946, the farm was appraised for the purpose of offering it for sale to satisfy William Edwin's instructions. Fortunately, two brothers, James and Mac, wished to remain on the property and were able to pay the appraised value, and the stipulated distribution was carried out. The final agreement between James and

Mac shows that James retained the family home and several acres, and the remaining acreage was divided equally between them. Both brothers spent the rest of their lives – Mac died in 1979 and James 2008 – on their beloved farm.

Leslie Oaks, the farm, was started in 1773 as the result of a land grant that was later reconfirmed when South Carolina became a state. A copy of the state reaffirmation document is shown in the appendix. This farm has been a very productive one over the years, providing resources that allowed the family a comfortable living, as well as a good education for the children.

When Thornwell Orphanage was opened at Clinton, S.C. after the War Between the States by a Presbyterian minister, the Leslies supported a good cause by donating farm products such as hams, flour, corn meal, oat meal, butter and other available produce. Even as late as the middle 1930's, a wagon loaded with barrels of those products left for Clinton at least once a year, and sometimes more often.

William Edwin was a forward-thinking individual, being one of the first to install 'indoor plumbing' by building a water tower that supplied pressure for the fixtures. He was also one of the first to install gas lighting by use of a generator, and owned an automobile before most of his neighbors. He became a 'master farmer' by attending seminars on various farm-related subjects and then seeing that the new methods or species were installed. His grandfather built a cotton gin which processed his own product as well as his neighbors', providing much needed cash. The Leslies were doing well until the boll weevil struck in the late 1920's, and soon after, the farm had to be mortgaged for the first time in its history.

With the death of William Edwin in 1939, and the loss of his guiding hand, the family struggled to keep the taxes and the yearly loan payments paid, though there were sons still at home. The combination of the weevil and the depression's twin attack made a difficult situation even more so, but between Mac, Robert and James the farm remained a going concern, though just by a hair. Hard work, scrimping on things that cost cash money, and bartering when they could, helped make it into the 1940's.

When the war opened up employment opportunities for the tenants, times really became tough. Mac left for the Navy, and James secured a cash-paying job with a local mill, leaving Robert to fight the battle by himself, or almost so, for James continued some 'off' time effort. A growing family meant that Robert had to not only worry about the taxes and loan payments, but also to provide the necessities of young children. This writer once remarked about hard farm work was from sunup to sundown, and Robert's reply was, "it isn't how hard it is, it's the seven day a week and fifty-two weeks a year with no break that's the hardest part." With cows to milk twice a day, fields to plow, crops to harvest, things to mend, wood to cut and split for the kitchen stove and fireplaces, animals to tend, shoeing for the horses and mules, (sometimes making the shoes in the workshop), shearing the sheep, slaughtering the hogs and lambs, preparing the hams for smoking – it seemed there was no end to it all for essentially one man. At one time five tenant families lived on the farm and there was always work for them. How Robert managed is a testament to his physical strength and determination to not let his mother down. Miss Annie died in 1946 and Robert didn't have the resources his brothers had achieved by working off the farm. It was an end to a lifestyle for him and many others in similar circumstances. Below is a schematic of the farm as it appeared just before the division between the brothers.

Legend

A. Main house
B. Well
C. Water tower
D. Chicken coop, pigeon roost
   smoke house
E. Garage
F. Shop
G. Cow barn
H. Syrup cooker
I. Slaughter area
J. Cane mill
K. Corn bin
L. Out house
M. Grain bin- oats/wheat
N. Garden
O. Hog lot
P. Horse/mule barn
Q. Equip. barn
R. Sheep barn
S. Tennant house
T. Tennant house
U. Cotton gin
V. Calhoun Creek
W. Tennis court
X. Spring head – water to tower
Y. Hwy. 28 – Anderson Rd.

The 1940's brought not only labor changes but also structural changes as well. The use and viability of the various buildings changed. The cotton gin ceased to operate in the 1920's, but the building remained, soon becoming dilapidated from lack of use and attention. Then as scrap iron was needed for the war effort, the steam engine was gone. The tennis court that William Edwin was so proud of reverted to its original condition. He enjoyed playing, but enjoyed seeing his children playing with their friends even more. The early experience that tennis court provided caused my father to enjoy the game so much he continued playing until his fifties, as did some of his brothers.

The first outbuilding to be demolished was the chicken coop/pigeon roost because of disuse, and the condition made it an eyesore. The second building to be eliminated was the equipment barn that served as a buggy shed in years when that vehicle was a necessity. It became dilapidated and was no longer needed. The sheep were sold off due to lack of available help, and sheep need a lot of attention, so that barn was also taken down. The water tower became obsolete when a new well was put into use, partly because the tower itself had begun to deteriorate, and the pump at the spring head needed constant attention. Of course, the well, with its windlass, was no longer needed, and it was eliminated when the old house burned down and a new one was built.

The car garage began the slow decline of an old building and rather than rebuild, it was eliminated. The shop building had originated in the 1800's as a part of the original house and was deemed unworthy of the necessary expense to maintain, and it was allowed to crumble. The corn crib was converted to a dairy in the latter part of the 1940's, where Robert established a small business in a desperate effort to earn a living and pay the taxes. The old barn started leaning and became unsafe even as a storage facility, and with no animals to house, it was unneeded and finally taken down. The cow barn suffered the same fate as did the old dairy building, but some storage facility was needed so James had a new metal building erected to replace the dairy. The only things left are the old outhouse, and it was kept more for a joke than anything else, and the cane mill.

When Ann and Franklin began spending more time at the farm to care for Ann's aging parents, Franklin had a building erected using the foundation of the barn, and has used it to house his woodworking shop where many beautiful creations have originated. Later a structure was built for storage on the site of the equipment barn, and just a few months ago, Franklin had a new barn built close to where the sheep barn had been. All the new structures have painted, metal siding and roofs in an effort to reduce maintenance and create longer lasting ones than the old wooden ones. Many other changes have been made to give the grounds a well-manicured appearance, and at the recent 2012 re-union, there were many remarks praising the way the place looks. Ann and Franklin renovated her parents' home, modernizing the interior, and have spent hours and much energy doing the same for the exterior. The whole place looks like someone really cares and loves the place – many plaudits to that couple.

Being a part of a working farm and its daily routines is a treasured experience. Those few years as a summer helper assisted in shaping a value system that has a great deal to do with the dedication to collect the necessary information and the desire to present the accumulated data as a tribute to those who created, maintained and preserved a family heritage that has lasted through the years. I am grateful for the opportunity afforded me by my personal family, as well as those of Robert, James and Mac to be in a position to gain this valuable experience.

As enjoyable as it was to see this dynamic exercise of what Thomas Jefferson so eloquently described as the most noble occupation man can be part of, it has been very painful to watch the inevitable change that has done away with that noble calling, as related to this property. This writer's father was fond of reminiscing about the life that started out in the horse and buggy world, and living to see a man walk on the moon. As an electrical engineer with over forty years working at AT&T, and being involved in many of their cutting edge technology projects, he realized how fortunate he was to be living in an age of unbelievable growth in knowledge and technical advancement. He also realized he was able to be part of that era as a contributor, because his father made sure his sons received the best education available, at least those older sons who matured before the decline of profitable farming. Of course, all that technological advancement was one of the prime movers in luring bright young people away from the farms to more glamorous careers in more glamorous locales and, thus, the death of small farming and rural lifestyles.

SOME REMINISCES

When this writer was five years old, his family made one of those weekend visits to his father's 'home place.' Before leaving for their Georgia home, the grandparents persuaded their son to let their youngest boy remain with them for the summer. What a wonderful summer – a weekend was never long enough to appreciate all the animals, new things to investigate, and the freedom to roam the barns, orchards and fields. The next summer it was a train ride to Abbeville and even more fun. Every summer after that was spent on the farm until an age was reached when the need for money was realized and summer jobs interfered with the ideal way to spend a summer.

A working farm has plenty of things to do – chores, uncles letting you think you were really helping, exploring the woods and creeks, and best of all - watching the work in the shop. If a part was needed to repair something, one of the uncles would go there and make it, sometimes firing up the charcoal smithy to heat metal so it could be pounded into shape, or using the drill press or other machines. It was fascinating, and I am sure that experience influenced my ability to make things in my own shop. My brother is using a wood lathe made by our father in that same shop as a teenager – using scrap iron for parts and old chisels and rasps for the cutting tools, learning that ability from necessity when he was tasked in keeping the cotton gin operating as a youngster. Spare parts and fittings were inaccessible most of the time and had to be made by hand, for the season of cotton ginning was short and downtime at the critical moment was not a good option.

Chickens were kept in the coop, but many roamed the yards and laid eggs wherever they wanted to, so when a chicken cackled, it was my job to find her and collect the eggs. A wood burning stove was used in the kitchen and needed a lot of wood, so the wood box needed attention every day before and after breakfast, lunch and dinner – my job.

38

The house actually had running water to fill the bathtub, but the drinking water was drawn from the well using a windlass. Two buckets were kept full, placed in different locations, each with a dipper, and someone had to draw the water – my job. It may sound dull, but it never was. A little reminder occasionally helped to keep those chores done on time, and no one was bashful about administering them. For the first few years, there was no electricity available, and a lighted kerosene lamp was necessary when bedtime arrived, but when I was about eleven, they not only got electricity, but also a telephone (a four-party line).

When aunts and uncles came for a weekend visit, there were always plenty of cousins devising some kind of games. Hay was stored in the barn loft by a big metal claw that was operated by horse power. A wagon load of hay was driven to the front of the barn, and the horses were un-hitched and connected to the claw by a rope. The claw ran along a track at the top of the loft, and when pulled to the end of the track, it dropped to the loaded hay wagon. The horses then pulled the claw up, and when reaching the track, it would slide along until the rope was jerked and the claw would release its load. This system allowed large piles of loose hay to accumulate and made perfect hills to play 'king on the mountain'.

Another favorite game was rotten egg fights. The sheep barn was so isolated that eggs were never collected from there, allowing them to re-main long enough to spoil. Getting hit by an egg didn't hurt, but those who were hit were required to go to the creek and wash off, for rotten-egg smell was not allowed in the house.

The creeks were available for swimming after enough rocks were col-lected to create a dam that would form a pond for youngsters to swim in. The only problem was, those ponds seemed to attract snakes, and after mentioning their presence at supper one night, the creek swimming holes were off limits. When cousins weren't available, tenant kids were, and all the same things attempted. We became good friends, but would never tussle – afraid they would hurt me probably. For those not aware of the situation, tenant farmers were almost always black families, and many ironic things happened in these close associations of young people.

The one event that has always stuck in my mind is the time three of us were involved in some activity – me and two black kids about my age. The details are a little fuzzy now, but for some reason the 'n' word was used toward one of the other kids. A pained expression appeared and he asked me not to use that word. Since it was not meant to be disrespectful, but just repeating a word I heard as a child, I asked what they would rather be called. The reply was, "just call us pickininnys (sic) or little black boys." When I related that to one of my uncles, he came down pretty hard on me, and to this day the 'n' word is never used.

One of the tenants was a family whose man of the house had died, but the mother and her several sons continued their long-time tenure on the farm. Janie, the mother, a very large woman, always wore a bandana on her head much like Scarlett O'Hara's Mammy in "Gone with the Wind." She helped out in the kitchen and was a wonderful cook, as well as a wonderful person – everybody loved Janie. She seemed to be part of the family, for after she became too old to function as she had as a younger woman and moved to town to live with one of her children, she always attended the family reunions and received a hug and a greeting from all the 'old hands'. From the very first summer spent on the farm, Janie was visited in the kitchen and got and received a big hug. She made the best egg custard pie ever tasted, and when she knew that a certain young man was due to arrive from Georgia, two egg custard pies were made – one for the family, and one for me – and put in the pie safe for leisurely enjoyment.

One of the chores expected of me when there for the summer was to go to the cow pasture and drive up the cows for their evening milking. The summer of my 11th year, everyone was busy when I arrived, and since it was time to go to the pasture for the cows, I just left without saying anything. The cow pasture covered a large area with several small, grassy patches and thick wooded areas in between. As I walked through one of the wooded areas, I could hear the cow bells, and it sounded like they were coming toward me, so I leaned against a tree to wait for them.

As the bells got louder, I thought they should be counted, so I turned toward the path and, to my shock and horror, the biggest Jersey bull I had ever seen was leading the line of cows down the path, and was only an arm's length from me, with his head lowered as if getting set to charge. The Jersey cow has black on her face and a little on her neck and the rest a tawny brown, but the Jersey bull is black all the way to his shoulders, with an imposing set of horns.

When my grandfather was alive (he died when I was eight), we would go all around the farm, with him holding my hand and explaining things, pointing out features and things that could be dangerous. One of the things he insisted on was that he would not go into a pasture where there was a bull without a pitchfork in his hand. I never saw him use the pitchfork on a bull, but he assured me that one of the reasons the bull stayed away from him was from a learned experience with the fork in the past. He wasn't afraid of the bulls, just held a healthy respect, and they were one of the dangerous things to be cautious about.

When I turned and saw that bull so close, the adrenalin rush was so great that I literally leaped to the lowest branch, watching the bull circle the tree looking up at me. (I tried later to reach that lower limb and couldn't even climb to it much less jump to it.) I waited in the tree till the cows had plenty of time to be well on their way to the barn, then got down and followed the path through the woods. The path took a sharp turn and when it was rounded, that huge bull was waiting for me, and I almost ran into his horns. There was no tree this time so I started running until I got to a barb wire fence and, without thinking, dove through it. Two of Janie's sons heard a strange noise that they said later sounded like a sick cow bellowing, and came to see what the problem was. With my clothes torn and blood flowing from several gashes, I was sitting on the ground, wailing away, scared out of my wits and thinking I was going to die in that field. The two boys picked me up and carried me to their house where Janie calmed me down, cleaned me up and told her sons to make sure I got to the 'big house'. Instead of consolation and concern, I got scolded by my uncle for running from his bull, thinking that my actions would cause him to be mean. After he convinced me the bull was very tame, without a mean streak, I put the idea to the test the next day. My uncle was right – that big brute loved to be patted, and scratching his left shoulder almost made him purr. I approached him many times that summer but still never really trusted him.

The next summer there was a promotion for me. When hay was cut it had to be raked into rows, making it easier to load. The rake had large, curved tines about six feet wide, pulled by a horse or mule, and had a lever that raised and lowered the tines. Learning to guide the horse, working the lever and keeping the line straight took some practice, but the uncles were patient and it finally came together. Later that summer when it was time to harvest the wheat and oats, my uncle rented a combine that required two people to operate – one person to drive and the other to sack the grain. As the grain was cut, the stalks and chaff were blown out the back, and the clean grain came down a chute with a 'y' that allowed two sacks to be pinned. You had to judge when the filling sack was almost full and pull a lever that diverted the grain to the other sack. The full sack was unpinned and tied with a hemp cord and thrown off the combine, and another empty sack pinned in its place. If you hustled, you had just enough time to process both sacks with little or no waste. It wouldn't have been so bad if it weren't for the chaff blowing on your hot, sweaty back, but at least you could contribute.

After the grain was combined, it had to be hauled to the mill, and the closest one was in Greenwood, about fifteen miles away. When the wagon was loaded, the mules had all they could handle, so it was a slow walk to the mill. The wait for the milled grain and the walk back was an all-day event, but at least I was able to handle the reins part of the way.

The last summer spent on the farm was my fifteenth year. A friend and I thought we had a job at a resort in North Carolina that summer, so we hitchhiked to the location, only to find that some accident caused them to close for repairs. With very little money, and no prospects of finding another job, we began to return to Georgia. When we finally reached Greenville, all the rides toward Atlanta disappeared. Standing on the side of the road in the hot sunshine, with our arms getting tired from holding them up with the thumb extended, I realized we were standing at a crossroad with one road leading to Abbeville. I told my friend we should try the other road to see if we had any luck there. Within a few minutes we got a ride to within three miles of the farm at Abbeville. I knew that, at least, we would find a good meal and friendly faces, but we found much more. A desperate Robert, in critical need of some help, had a smile a mile wide when we announced that we were looking for something to do for the rest of the summer. We made one big mistake though. My friend casually mentioned that we were on the high school football team and would like to get in shape for our soph-omore year. Needless to say, Robert made absolutely sure we were in the best condition of our entire lives.

My friend had never been on a farm, so spending over two months on one is something he still talks about – over seventy years later, it truly was a lot of fun. We were old enough and big enough to really be a help to Robert, and it was a crowning experience for me, learning to enjoy a large part of my heritage. We didn't earn any money that summer, but we were fed well and got a lot of exercise, and were ready to play football when we returned home.

Chapter Five

THE FAMILY

Thomas – b. 1725, d. 1778. Unfortunately, the life of Thomas is shrouded in mystery for there is no written record of his existence beyond the recording of his land grant in 1766. He was responsible for establishing the Lesslie farm along Calhoun Creek, part of which remains in the control of his descendant's today. His sons, William and Thomas, assisted him in creating a productive and profitable enterprise from the raw frontier that existed when they arrived from Northern Ireland. That frontier continued to be such for many years while the scattered settlers of the area strived to clear enough arable land that could grow crops sufficient to sustain their families. At the same time, an effort was made to establish numbers of livestock – horses, cattle, swine, sheep, chickens and other animals that are necessary for a self-sufficient existence. The plentiful existence of wild animals, such as wolves, bears and panthers, in the forests reduced the pioneers' efforts along this line, and always presented a menace to the maintenance of their domesticated farm critters. Barns were necessary to protect their animals, especially at night, and the labor to create them and other outbuildings must have been extraordinarily difficult, since one had to create all the building materials needed, as well as the erection labor. Fortunately, the forests provided all the raw materials needed. It seems strange that no record of his death exists.

A land grant map shows some of the Abbeville area features relative to this narrative: (1) the locations of the land grants of Thomas and John Lesly in relation to present landmarks, (2) Andrew Pickens' Block House – built as a place of refuge in times of strife such as Indian attacks. During the Revolutionary War, a powder magazine was built nearby. (3) the site of Long Cane Cemetery that Thomas and John began. (On their voyage to America, the brothers, realizing that the kind of environment they were heading for would possibly produce injuries and early deaths, and that their bounty land grants were not likely to be adjacent, agreed to establish a 'burying ground' between their new homes. Note that the cemetery is almost exactly half way between the two properties.) (4) the William Lesly farm – an irregular shaped property that was unusual for this period, since almost all newly surveyed properties were laid out as squares or rectangles as seen on the diagram on the following page. This was obviously a property that was fitted in between existing surveyed and recorded ones. (5) the Josiah Martin tract that was transferred to Thomas Lesly in 1785 (Thomas, son of Thomas). Note the location of the Thomas Lesslie property in relation to the Burt-Stark Mansion. Family tradition maintains David Lesly built this house on property owned by his family, and only slight adjustment of the grant lines would be necessary to include the site of that house. Richard K. McMurtry is responsible for the creation of the land grant map used to portray the locations cited above. In his Guide to the Map of Colonial and Early Statehood Settlers of Calhoun Creek, Long Cane Settlement, Abbeville and McCormick Counties, South Carolina, page 2, paragraph 4, "The boundaries of each plat and its location on the modern day map are approximations. Some plats may be within 10 or 20 feet of their actual location. Others may be as much as 500 feet different than depicted. This is because of inaccuracies in the plats as recorded or inaccuracies in the survey itself. Some parcels, even when the plats suggested that the parcels had a common boundary, had slightly different bearings on the plats or seemed to overlap or be separated by a distance. However, despite these inaccuracies, in most cases, the locations are fairly accurate."

Plotting ancient surveys that were done with relatively crude instruments, at least by today's standards, is a task that is inherently difficult to attain absolute accuracy, as Mr. McMurtry states above, but is far superior to any alternative. The absence of recorded real estate transactions in this area due to loss caused by fire, makes this type of plotting of otherwise unmanageable land ownership locations a true godsend for those interested in their families' landed estates of past times. It would be ideal to be able to determine the deposition of the acres granted to Thomas, but, lacking the means to resolve such a chore, a little deduction and sense of the normal progression of events in a growing area would indicate a gradual sell-off of small parcels until the entire acreage is absorbed by growth.

Another family tradition would account for a portion of the Thomas Lesslie grant. The oldest surviving son of William, son of Thomas, was James, who became a lawyer, and practiced that profession in the village of Abbeville until his untimely death in 1808. James married Eliza Bird two years previous to his death and built a house close to the house his younger brother, David, would build (Burt-Stark Mansion), evidently using land that was part of his grandfather's grant.

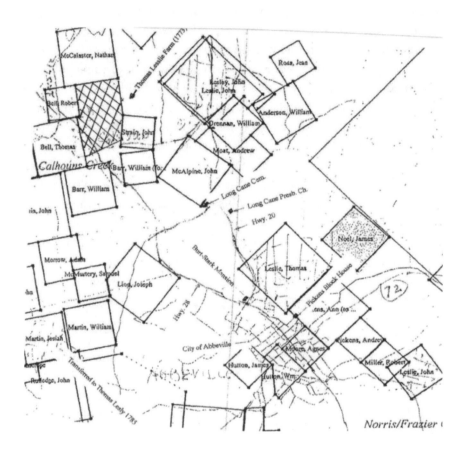

GENERATION TWO

The children of Thomas and Jane Lesslie

1.1 – William – b. Nov. 10, 1754, d. Dec.30, 1821. He arrived in Charleston, age 11, from Country Antrim Northern Ireland. According to Scotch-Irish tradition, he would have received an education from at least his Presbyterian Kirk and possibly from district schools, although Presbyterians were severely limited because of their 'dissenter' status imposed by the Church of Ireland. At age nineteen, he helped his father establish a farm on over six hundred acres, and at thirty, began a surveying activity that he maintained throughout his lifetime.

In 1778 he married Ann Caldwell, daughter of James and Elizabeth Harris Caldwell. James was an immigrant from County Donegal, Northern Ireland; she was from Anson County North Carolina. William and Ann had eleven children – eight sons and three daughters. Ann died at age forty-one and William remarried a 'Miss Lesly' and they had one son. Since both William and Patrick Calhoun married Caldwell ladies, and both men were surveyors, there seems to be some confusion about a connection of the two families. William's Ann was from the Abbeville area, and Patrick's wife was from the Newberry area. Both families and their backgrounds have been examined, and there is no apparent connection of the two – two different families entirely, just a lot of similarities.

The Ninety-Six District was established in 1769 and its first courthouse built in 1772. "A few years later, its population having increased, the old Ninety-Six District was divided into six districts. Provisions were made for each of these districts to have its own seat of government. A committee was appointed in each district for the purpose of naming the district and selecting the site of its seat of government. The appointed members, in what later became

Abbeville District, were Dr. De La Howe, Hugh Wardlaw, Major Hamilton, William Leslie and Mr. Alston."[7] This action was actually taken in 1783.

William was active in the Long Cane Presbyterian Church, one of only three in the upper part of the state which continues by that name today. In 1793, William helped establish the Long Cane Society to provide a permanent fund for such benevolent purposes as support for orphans, a supplemental fund for ministers' expenses, and care and upkeep of Long Cane Cemetery. He left funds in his will to continue support for this Society, and it continues to be active in its original purposes today.

In 1813, William was instrumental in the building of a new house of worship. "Trustees of the Congregation for this purpose were William Lesley (sic), Hugh Reid, George Bowie, Matthew Wilson, and James Wardlaw."[8] The Presbyterian heritage his ancestors helped to establish in Scotland, and continued in Ireland, was an important part of the lives of their descendants. All of his children were members of this church, but his son, David, was to follow more closely in his footsteps, becoming a leading elder.

In 1784 William, after serving a short time as an apprentice, struck out on his own and began surveying properties in the district, soon becoming one of the most active in Ninety-Six District. With over 400 surveys signed by him and recorded in state Archives over a 37-year career, William ranks in comparison to Patrick Calhoun, one of the first surveyors in the district, acting in that capacity for his father's land grant in 1766. The profession of surveying requires knowledge of properties adjacent to those being surveyed in order to identify those landowners as a part of his official survey. This knowledge evidently led to the acquisition of unclaimed land to be used as additional farms, or other uses. Patrick Calhoun is known to have left five separate farms to his heirs at his death.

---

[7] Abbeville County Family History by Lester Ferguson, page 5

[8] Keeping the Faith, A History of Upper Long Cane Presbyterian Church by Mrs. Pearl M. Stevenson, page 12

It appears from the records that William also began speculating in land. When the Cherokee Indians ceded more property, creating what is now Anderson County, records show William either surveyed, or had surveyed for him, four 1000-acre tracts in the space of a few months. It appears he obtained these tracts to sell at a later date, though he did accumulate many acres. His last will shows that he gave his daughter, Ann, 600 acres, his son, William, the 650-acre farm he lived on, and at an earlier date, his son, John Harris, enough property for him to be considered a planter, as well as acreage to his son, Robert Hall. The inventory of his estate at his death in 1821 also shows a high degree of business acumen in his bookkeeping ability. The list of money due him for surveying activity includes a debt from John Campbell for $2.50 from 1792, and one from John Cain for $1 from 1804.

William obviously considered education very important since he saw that his sons received all they desired – two lawyers, a medical doctor, a school teacher, two surveyors, and a successful planter. He even provided funds to continue the education of his three youngest sons in his will; one of those became one of the lawyers, one the medical doctor, and the other the school teacher.

William died a very respected citizen of the community, fulfilling all the dreams he could possibly have brought with him from Northern Ireland – a true frontiersman, business man, devoted Christian, active in his community, and an original American patriot. The list of executors of his last will is probably a good indication of the esteem he enjoyed among his contemporaries, for it includes many of the leading men of the area. (See appendix.)

1.2 – Margaret – b. 1756 - ? The only record of her continued existence is acreage surveyed for her by her brother, William, in the 1780's, in what is now Anderson County.

1.3 – Thomas – b. 1760, d. Feb. 22, 1839. Arrived in Charleston at age 5. The information was acquired from a copy of a deposition by Thomas in 1832, in an effort to claim Revolutionary War pension. (See appendix). He was living in McMinn County, Tennessee at the time.

He stated that he was born in County Antrim, Ireland, joined state militia under command of Capt. Joseph Pickens about 1777 at father's farm in Abbeville, chased Tory named McGirt, returned to residence which was place of rendezvous, then in action against Cherokees, was released and rejoined in mounted unit under Col. Andrew Pickens where he saw action at Cowpens. He was then sent to Georgia in search of Tories and was ordered to take no prisoners and not spare any that needed killing. Shortly after the war he moved to Pendelton, S.C. where he married Mary Harris, and their union produced nine children. They later moved to Tennessee.

1.4 – Jane – b. 1763 -?   No record has been found for her.

GENERATION THREE

(Grandchildren of Thomas and Jane Lesslie)

The children of William and Ann Caldwell Lesly

1.1.1 – Thomas – b. May 12, 1780, d. July 3, 1784.

1.1.2 – James – b. Aug. 8, 1780, d. Aug. 9, 1808. Became a lawyer, married and had one daughter, Francis Caroline, born after his death. A doctor named Bushnell or Bochelle, depending on the source, made a disparaging remark about one of James' relatives while treating him, and harsh words were exchanged which led to blows that led to a challenge by the doctor. James had no choice but acceptance of the challenge, and a duel was fought with pistols on a sand bank on the Georgia side of the Savannah River. The first fires of both were misses, and an agreement to suspend was sought, but the doctor refused. James was shot in the chest and died several hours later. His wife was told of the impending duel by a servant and hurriedly rushed to the scene, only to arrive too late. James wrote out his will before leaving for the fateful encounter, and even mentioned a debt to the doctor that would have been difficult to prove otherwise. His wife moved to Georgia where their daughter met James Van Ness and later married him. They moved to New Orleans and later to San Francisco where he became mayor. James built a house, either before his marriage or shortly after, on land, history maintains, belonged to family along present day Greenville Street and, after his death, was used as the Presbyterian manse. Francis Caroline visited Abbeville and was mentioned in Lowry Ware's book about Olde Abbeville. A.E. L. mentions receipt of a letter from Eliza B. Van Ness in his diary of 1859.

1.1.3 – John Harris – b. Feb. 11, 1784, d. July 31, 1855. (Maternal grandmother's maiden name was Harris.) Married Mary Gilliland at age 18, given property in the Due West area that was previously used as second home by parents, evidently was successful farmer/planter. Apparently had a disagreement with father who left him a Shorter Catechism in will with instructions to study two questions, both of which had to do with sin. His wife's family had a reputation of being rabidly antislavery, and John, Mary and family left South Carolina for Indiana in the 1830's with a group of abolitionists. John had difficulty establishing his family in that state and moved to Alabama, living close to his sister, Ann, the rest of his life. He and Mary had 10 children.

1.1.4 – Jane – b. Feb. 1, 1786, d. Aug. 2, 1807. Died unmarried. She and a younger sister died of a fever, thought to emanate from the gristmill pond. Her brother, Robert, was suspected of destroying the dam that created the pond in his despondency, but evidently was never pursued, and remained on good terms with family, even though the grist mill was incapacitated.

1.1.5 – Robert Hall – b. 14, 1787, d. April 9. In 1847, he married Elizabeth Watt, daughter of an Irish immigrant, Samuel Watt and his wife, Janet Lesly. Janet was the daughter of John Lesly, one of the two original immigrant brothers. Robert was given part of his father's estate that was across the road from his homestead. He established a farm and later purchased additional acreage to the Southeast. When his brother, David, began a farm on 95 acres abutting his northeast property line, it provided Lesly land ownership along the south side of what is now Hwy. 28 for almost three miles. David sold his 95-acre farm to Nicholas Miller, who became the father-in-law of A.E. Lesly, in 1850.

The original Robert Lesly land was in family ownership until the 1960's. Robert was not only a planter/farmer, but also an avid horseman, known throughout the area for his fine breed of riding and carriage horses. He was fond of exhibiting the quality of his horses, as well as his horsemanship. His sons, James and John Watt, had the pleasure of displaying those qualities when they each went to Columbia College, now University of South Carolina. Robert built a home as his homestead in 1809, and that house stands today, occupied by a family that enjoys the antiquity of their home. It is one of the oldest houses in the county. See below as the house looks today. This is one of three houses that were built in the 1800's by sons of William, and all three remain in good condition today. Robert's brother, David, built the other two. Robert, like his father and brother, William, com-bined farming with the practice of surveying and, evidently, was very successful at both. Robert and Elizabeth had eight children, six sons and two daughters.

1.1.6 – Elizabeth – b. Dec. 1, 1789, d. Aug. 17, 1807. Died of fever, unmarried – see Jane above.

1.1.7 – Ann – b. Nov. 7, 1791, d. Jan. 4, 1863. Married a neighbor, Samuel Jack, moved to Alabama and established a farm, no children. Her brother, John Harris, joined her in Talladega County, Alabama on an adjoining farm after moving initially to Indiana.

1.1.8 – William – b. April 25, 1793, d. Feb. 9, 1867. In 1827, he married Martha Emily White, continuing to live in the house of his birth, and upon his father's death, inherited the 650-acre farm he grew up on. He continued a successful farming operation as well as practicing his father's profession of surveying. After the loss of the family gristmill and its income, partly to replace the missing income and partly because cotton had become the money crop, William built a cotton gin that processed his farm's cotton as well as neighbors'. It is not known whether the original gin used a steam engine as its power source or it was added later, but in his son's diary of 1859, mention is made of a mule-powered gin owned by his brother-in-law, Lemuel Reid, and it is possible this gin was also originally that way. The gin would continue in profitable operation until the 1930's, and remains of the original building could be seen as late as 2008.

William continued the Leslie tradition of being an active Presbyte-rian in his support of the Long Cane Church and of the Long Cane So-ciety. He evidently was also active in civic affairs for he and his neighbor, Samuel Jack, were responsible for tracking down and capturing Payton Randolph after he murdered James Kyle in his store on the town square.

At the end of the War Between the States, Abbeville was host to Confederate President Davis and cabinet members, Sec. of War Breckinridge, Post Master Reagan, Sec. of Navy Mallory, and Sec. of State Benjamin. It was a short, hurried stop in a rush to get beyond Federal patrols and either out of the country or the Trans-Mississippi and safety (Texas). During their stay, the local citizens had a chance to meet those esteemed gentlemen, mingling with them during a period of comparative relaxation from the tension of their journey from Richmond. Their primary concern was the safety of the President, but each member also had to consider how and what provisions they must make for their own welfare.

Judah P. Benjamin, who was considered the most intelligent member of the Confederate government and the most gregarious among them, was seeking special information that would assist him in planning his own attempt at survival. When the entourage departed Abbeville about midnight, most of the government officials rode in military wagons and ambulances escorted by several cavalry troops, except Benjamin and a few others who were horseback. Benjamin, not being accustomed to being in the saddle, purchased an old buggy soon after crossing the Savannah River. He continued his journey in more comfort to some place in Florida where a boat could be procured that would facilitate his escape. Col. Leovy, a fellow Louisianan, traveling on horseback with him as a companion and interpreter for Benjamin, posed as a Frenchman who could speak no English. They headed Southwest across Georgia, and when the pair crossed the Florida line, Col. Leovy left his companion to travel west toward Louisiana. Benjamin found James Thomas Leslie at his Madison, Florida plantation and was provided information that would lead him to James' brother, Leroy Gilliland Lesley (note spelling change) in Brooksville, Florida. After Madison, he assumed the role of someone looking for land, wearing simple homespun clothes provided by James' wife, Mary.

William Lesly was the only person in Abbeville with knowledge of his nephews in Florida, for his younger brother, Samuel, was living with his nephew, Leroy, at the time. William and his younger brother maintained regular communications with each other. For more description of the events involving the Confederate officials at that time, see below in the discussion of William's brother, David, and his nephew, Leroy.

Even though farming was the activity of a vast majority of the population and usually a prosperous enterprise, cash money was always in short supply. The practice of surveying had several advantages, one of which was collection in cash for their services, for specie was in short supply nationally, and anyone in possession of it had a great deal of flexibility. In William's case, it allowed him to provide his sons with a good education. William and Martha Lesly had six children, four living to adulthood.

1.1.9 – Thomas – b. June 15, 1795, d. April 14, 1829. Little is known about this son except that he became a medical doctor and selected New Orleans to establish his practice where he died in one of the many fever epidemics that swept that city in the early days. He apparently died unmarried.

1.1.10 – David – b. June 15, 1797, d. Feb. 6, 1854. One of the most outstanding men of the area in his day – lawyer, judge, builder, church leader, temperance promoter, farmer. He married Louisa Kyle, daughter of James Kyle (murdered by Payton Randolph while standing in his store on the town square.) David and Louisa had no children to survive, but her niece, Jane McWhorther, lived with them until she married David's nephew, John Watt Lesly.

In 1839, David built a house on land bordering the farm of his brother, Robert H., and lived there until 1850 when he sold the house and 95 acres to Nicholas Miller who raised his family there that included, among others, two daughters who would have significant connection to the Lesly family. One daughter, Virginia was to marry David's nephew, Alpheus E. Lesly, this writer's great-grandfather. Thus David, a great-great uncle, built the house and sold it to a great-great-grandfather. A second daughter, Ann, married James S. Stark and they bought a second house that David built, the Burt-Stark Mansion. Both houses remain today in beautiful condition, though neither is occupied.

The first house is shown below as it looked in 1893 when John L. Hill purchased the house and ninety-five acres. The house had been neglected by the previous owner and was in an advanced state of dilapidation as can be seen.

The Hill family began a renovation project that not only restored it, but also vastly improved the interior, but more importantly, transformed the exterior into a truly beautiful southern residence. Over the years improvements were continued, and today it appears as shown below.

The house was occupied until a few years ago, but is now used as a center piece for special occasions such as weddings, reunions, Christmas Open House events, etc.

A family connection is mentioned above, regarding the original builder and the first purchaser, Nickolas Miller, and there is also a family connection between the Leslies and the Hills. Alpheus E. Lesly married Nickolas Miller's daughter, and his son, William Edwin, married a descendant of the Hill family who purchased it in 1893 – one of the many 'cousin connections' of a small southern community.

The second house that David built is now known as the Burt-Stark Mansion. It was also allowed to fall into disrepair and was purchased by James S. Stark who restored it. His daughter, Mary Davis, at the age of 102, willed the house and property to the Abbeville Historical Society and is now used as a tourist attraction, opened on weekends and special occasions.

This house has an interesting background from two standpoints. The first instance is the house's conception and how it was built; the second instance is that an important historical event occurred in and around the house.

While David and Louisa were living in their first house they took an extended vacation to the Northeast. On an excursion along the Hudson River Valley they saw a house they both admired. They returned to Abbeville shortly after that and David decided to reproduce that house as closely as he could. To make sure he would be able to incorporate the details that made it so attractive, he sent a slave named Cubie, or Cubic, on horseback to its site to make sketches and record the proper dimensions. Cubie returned and acted as David's foreman and lead carpenter in the construction process, using material cut from his lands, including the walnut used on the interior. No records have been found to corroborate the timetable, but two known facts would indicate that it was probably started in 1846 to 1847. First David was not shown in the 1850 census to be a town resident, and if he had resided in this house, he would be qualified. Second, we have the contract between David and Nicholas Miller in 1850. At this time in history, residential construction required components such as moldings, door and window casings and other specialty items to be made on site by carpenters and joiners. Since most of the interior finish material is walnut, a very hard wood not easily worked with hand tools, two or three years would not be an unreasonable completion period.

At the time of the above construction David was a judge, attorney, and a farmer or planter, a term that was used extensively at the time, probably to denote a social step above the ordinary farmer. He also played an important role in building a brick sanctuary across the street from his new house for those Presbyterians living in town.

David was the first non-ministerial commissioner to represent the South Carolina Presbytery in the General Assembly, and remained a very active elder in the Upper Long Cane Presbyterian Church until his death. The depth of his faith contributed to his being elected to the city council on a 'no license ticket', meaning that no license to sell liquor would henceforth be approved. When the reality of no licensed public liquor sales appeared, a so-called 'whiskey war' broke out, and the incident that brought it to a close was described by Addison F Posey in Dr. Lowry Ware's book, "Old Abbeville, Scenes of the Past of a Town Where Old Time Things Are Not Forgotten". Mr. Posey relates the acts of the 'wets' and the 'drys' that led up to a decision of the 'wets' they hoped would be a final solution to their problem. The 'wets' held a meeting where it was decided that one of the leading 'dry' advocates would be assaulted and thereby convince the town council of their seriousness. As the council members were mentioned as a possible victim, each was rejected for various reasons. The last member was David Lesley (sic) and his stature being only medium and in his late forties, he was picked to be that victim. A $10 bill was offered to anyone willing to take up the task, and the largest of the group snatched up the bill and headed for the Court House, in front of which Judge Lesly was standing with a dozen others.

The first hint of trouble was a blow delivered by a Goliath to the Judge's jaw that staggered him. Recovering, the Judge struck the assailant a blow to the pit of the stomach, which totally overthrew him, and the next moment saw Goliath with David astride him and pressing his throat almost to strangulation. The excited crowd tendered him opened knives and insisted on his cutting his throat or cropping his assailant, but the Judge's magnanimity prevailed and he arose, inviting his opponent to arise and go.

The second instance of importance regarding this house occurred eleven years after David's death, in 1865. David's widow, Louisa, sold the house after David's death, and after two owners occupied it, a former U.S. Representative, Armistead Burt, purchased it. While in Washington Mr. and Mrs. Burt became close friends with the Jefferson Davises. As the War Between the States was coming to a close, Varina Jefferson took their children out of Richmond by train with the intention of reaching their Mississippi home. On the way, she stopped at Abbeville and stayed a week with her old friends, the Burt's. The news of roving Union patrols in the area caused a fear that her presence might spur the Union forces to burn her friend's house, compelling her to leave to begin her journey to Mississippi.

As the final days of the Confederacy were approaching, Jefferson Davis also left Richmond, along with the remaining Cabinet members, and traveled as far as possible by train, but at this stage of the war, tracks had been destroyed in scattered locations, so they continued on horseback and in wagons when necessary. Several contingents of cavalry were added to the entourage as a protective force when the tracks became impassable. The President finally reached Abbeville, expecting to meet his family, but the delays caused a missed connection. Mr. Davis spent the remainder of the day with the Burt's, and while there held meetings with his Generals and Cabinet members in the Burt parlor. These meeting are considered the last Confederate War Council meeting. A few days after leaving Abbeville, the Davis party was captured by Union patrols.

1.1.11 – Ezekiel – b. March 1, 1799, d. Oct., 1809.

1.1.12 – Samuel Watt – this son was the issue of a second marriage, a Miss Lesly that historians failed to record any information about. Samuel became a teacher and moved in the 1850's to Tampa, Fla. and lived with a nephew, Leroy, son of John Harris.

GENERATION FOUR
(Great-grandchildren of Thomas and Jane Lesslie)
(Grandchildren of William and Ann Caldwell Lesly)

The child of James and Eliza Bird Lesly

1.1.2.1 – Francis Caroline – b. 1808. Married James Van Ness who became Mayor of San Francisco. She and her son, Tom, visited Abbeville sometime after 1850 and stayed with her uncle David. Francis Caroline and James had two children.

The children of John Harris and Mary Gilliland Lesly

1.1.3.1 – William Alexander – b. Sept. 21, 1805.

1.1.3.2 – Leroy Gilliland – b. May 11, 1807, d. Oct. 31, 1882. Married Indianna Chiles Livingston May 1, 1834. She was an Abbeville native, b. April 22, 1809. He and his younger Brother, James, moved to Madison, Florida around 1834, a time of turmoil in the South and particularly in the Abbeville area. The momentum and Leroy's mother, Mary Gilliland, was a member of a family that professed almost rabid sentiments along that line. A large group of people from the surrounding area was moving to the Midwest and Leroy's parents were among the group, choosing Indiana as their future home.

Evidently Leroy and his brother, James, either did not share the radical views of their parents, or chose to follow other area residents to Florida, an area recently obtained from Spain and in the process of gaining U.S. territorial status. Among the families that preceded them were the Livingston's, for soon after settling in Madison, Leroy married Indiana Livingston.

Both Leroy and James established plantations and began the lives of planters which James continued to pursue, but after only a few years, Leroy felt the call of the ministry and qualified to be a Methodist circuit-riding minister, covering northern Florida and southern Georgia. The Methodist Church soon transferred him to the Tampa area where he established several churches and a reputation as a rousing minister.

When the indigenous Indian tribes allied with the Seminoles began attacking the scattered Florida settlers, causing death and destruction, militia units were organized to protect the citizens and chastise the offenders. Leroy volunteered his services and soon was elevated to the status of Captain in charge of one of the units. Leroy's brother, James, was soon recruited, and together they established a reputation the Indians feared and respected. Both served in different periods of Indian activity as the situation required and had many close encounters that could have resulted in death.

An interesting event occurred during this period, but was known only after the Seminoles were defeated and peace was restored. It seems that Leroy was leading a patrol of mounted militia through the dense undergrowth that covered that particular area in an effort to find one of the primary Seminole chiefs, known as Billy Bowlegs. To Leroy's credit, his experience had taught him to deploy outriders on both sides of the main force to guard against surprise attacks. Bowlegs' band had camouflaged their position as only wily Indians could, and remained unseen as the troops passed his hiding place. As Billy related some years later, he was prepared to spring his surprise on Leroy, who by that time was a well-known figure to the Indians, when he realized the outriders where within sight. To save himself and his tribesmen for another day, Leroy was allowed to continue his patrol. It has been reported that Billy told this story to the superior officer of the state militia forces with much glee, laughing and slapping his thighs as he related the details of how he almost killed the famous Leroy Lesley.

The period known as the Seminole Indian War was not one specific time, but several that saw times of intense fighting and then times of relative peace. The Indians would take to the war path again and reaction to their depredations brought peace treaties, only to be broken again. The War finally ended in 1858, with many of the Seminoles being removed to the Oklahoma Territory. Each time militia units were needed in the field, Leroy and James were in the saddle and in the areas where they were needed most.

Soon after defeating the Indian menace, the War Between the States broke out and Leroy again took to the saddle, leading an effort to protect coastal areas from Union invasion. Between stints of those patrols, he rounded up the open range cattle and drove them to railheads for Confederate commissaries.

When the War Between the States ended, Leroy was preparing for a period of peace and quiet at his plantation north of Tampa near the town of Brooksville when a stranger knocked on his door. The man was portly and dressed in old clothes that gave him an air of one down on his luck. The man introduced himself as Charles Howard, but when Leroy acknowledged his identity, the stranger changed his demeanor and disclosed his true identity as Judah Benjamin. Leroy knew instantly to whom he was talking, for his visitor was well known to those active in the Confederate cause. After the initial shock of having such a famous individual at his door, Leroy offered him a true Southern welcome, making him as comfortable as possible. A bath, some clean clothes, a full meal and a little rest brought out Benjamin's gregarious nature and an explanation of his unannounced arrival and how he happened to find the person he was looking for. He relayed greetings from his Abbeville relatives and brother, James.

The reason he was there was simple – he needed help to get out of the country before Federal Patrols found him and certain prison. He explained his trip from Abbeville, through Georgia and to Madison, and was led to believe Leroy was the person capable of finding a method to affect his escape. He found very quickly that Leroy was not only capable but more than willing to do what was necessary to see him safely on his way.

After receiving assurance of help and the normal southern hospitality, a bath, some fresh clothes and a home cooked meal, Mr. Benjamin reverted to his normal affable personality and regaled the family with a repertoire of humorous stories, including tales of his travel through Georgia and Florida. Leroy's son, John Thomas, had been a Major in the Confederate Cavalry and retained a relationship with his former unit known as the Cow Calvary. That unit had been formed late in the war to protect the state's range cattle from Federal raiding parties, as well as rustler activity. One last assignment included getting Mr. Benjamin around Federal check points to a location south of Tampa that would allow better opportunities of finding a ship that could take him to either the Bahamas or Cuba. The Gamble Mansion in Ellington, close to the Manatee River, was chosen as a safe haven, and that site was later named the Judah P. Benjamin Memorial for its vital role in securing Benjamin's safe evacuation. After several harrowing adventures, Benjamin finally reached England where he became a famous Barrister.

1.1.3.3 – Moses Taggart – b. April 5, 1809.

1.1.3.4 – Theodore Josephus – b. Jan. 30, 1811, d. 1890. He evidently lived close to his Aunt Ann Lesly Jack near Talladega, Alabama and was partly responsible for his parents' move from Indiana to Alabama. He married Rebecca Brock and they had thirteen children.

1.1.3.5 – James Thomas – b. March 13, 1813, d. Aug. 24, 1897. He moved to Madison, Florida with brother, Leroy, in the 1830's and later served with him in state militia units. He was involved in many skirmishes with Indian bands, coming close to death on occasions. He applied for a pension offered by the U.S. Government to survivors of the Seminole War and was required to execute an affidavit (see appendix) in which he stated that he changed the spelling of his name from Lesly to Leslie because he thought it looked prettier than his brother's change to Lesley, called his grandfather, William, an old Irishman, and related a visit to a cousin (child of Robert Hall) in Pontotoc, Miss. That Madison farm remains in family hands, and this writer has sampled some tasty watermelons from there. The family continues to remain in touch through frequent reunions. James Thomas married Mary Sever July, 1842, and they had seven children.

1.1.3.1 – Madison Livingston – b. 1844.

1.1.3.2 – Dicy Priscilla – b. 1846.

1.1.3.3 – Moses – b. April 2, 1849.

1.1.3.4 – Lewis Gilliland – b. 1851.

1.1.3.5 – Charles – b. 1854.

1.1.3.6 – William Sever – b. Aug. 10. 1855.

1.1.3.7 – Mary Indianna – b. Sept. 22, 1856.

The children of Robert Hall and Elizabeth Watt Lesly

1.1.4.1 – Jane Ann – b. Dec. 10, 1810, d. June 25, 1898. She married John Glenn Fraser, but had no children. They adopted Eliza Lulah, the daughter of her brother, James Lewis, and raised her when James' wife, Eliza Wilson, died. John Glenn died in 1840 leaving Jane Ann to raise their adopted child alone. Eliza Lulah married James White and they had two daughters. When Eliza Lulah died shortly after the birth of her second daughter, Jane Ann adopted and raised those young girls as well. She spent her later years at the home of a relative, Annie White Reid.

This lady was a Lesley to be proud of for she was remembered fondly and with much love by those who knew her. She exhibited qualities of an indomitable spirit that exceeded those of most humans.

1.1.4.2 – James Lewis – b. Oct. 12, 1812, d. July 14, 1891. He married Eliza Wilson who died shortly after the birth of their first child, Eliza Lulah. She was adopted by his sister and raised by her. He married, secondly, Charlotte Mantague Watkins and had five children. James Lewis was a graduate of Colombia College, now the University of South Carolina. He taught school in Greenwood and later was President of Cokesbury College in what is now Greenwood County. After the War in 1865, he retired from teaching and farmed the rest of his life.

1.1.4.3 – Samuel – b. March 19, 1815. He married against his family's wishes for his new wife was a family governess, Mary Ann Price. It must have proved to be a dilemma not easily solved for they moved to Pontotoc, Mississippi where they lived on a large cotton plantation. He evidently stayed in touch with family for his cousin, James Thomas, son of John Harris, while living in Florida, visited him there.

1.1.4.4 – William Andrew – b. Oct. 5, 1817. He married Virginia White and they had no children.

1.1.4.5 – John Watt – b. Dec. 6, 1819, d. April 24, 1892. He married Louisa Jane McWhorter, niece of Louisa Lesly, and the wedding was held at David and Louisa's new home, now known as the Burt-Stark Mansion. He, like his brother, James Lewis, was a graduate of Colombia College. He was a sergeant in The War Between the States and was wounded several times, finally losing an arm. He learned to do normal farm chores without the arm on the farm he inherited from his father. John Watt and Louisa had seven children.

1.1.5.6 – Robert L. – b. May 1, 1822, d. Sept. 25, 1823.

1.1.5.7 – Cornelia – b. Aug. 25, 1824, d. Nov. 1833.

1.1.5.8 – Thomas Harris – b. Oct. 7, 1828, d. Feb. 24, 1862. Thomas evidently acted as his Aunt Louisa's overseer on the farm she continued to own after David's death. He was killed while in the Confederate Army.

The children of William and Martha Emily White Lesly

1.1.8.1 – Anna Louisa – b. Oct. 7, 1828, d. July 14, 1859. She married Col. Jesse Ward Norris. They lived in Anderson County near his father. They had two daughters.

1.1.8.2 – Augustus – b. July 26, 1830, died in infancy.

1.1.8.3 – Virginia Elizabeth – b. Jan. 30, 1832, d. Nov. 17, 1903. She married James Archibald Montgomery. He was a farmer and school teacher. They lived in Anderson County and had six children.

1.1.8.4 – Alpheus Ezekiel – b. Feb. 2, 1834, d. March 23, 1905. In 1862, he married Virginia Miller, b. Aug. 15, 1839, d. April 1892. Alpheus, known to family and friends as A.E., and his brother, John J., inherited their father's farm jointly. A.E. later bought his  brother's interest and continued to live on the farm his entire life. As a 25-year old, he kept a diary in which he described his activities and those of the farm workers and their activities, as well as the current weather conditions. That diary has been transcribed and footnoted to explain connections of the people he mentions and, as far as possible, their social and/or family affiliation. His uncle, Lemuel Reid, his mother's brother and neighbor, also kept a diary of the following year, and will be mentioned during this narrative.

The 1850 census listed A.E. as a student and it is evident he was fairly well educated by the way he described things and by his handwriting. It is not known where he obtained his schooling, but Erskine College is only 12 miles from his residence and it is known that his cousins, sons of his Uncle Lemuel, attended that school. He joined a local militia group in 1860 and met with them on a regular basis for instruction and practice and, according to Lemuel's 1860 diary, borrowed money to buy a uniform. The following year, as war talk became more prevalent, his unit was marched to Charleston and was encamped on Sullivan's Island when Fort Sumter was fired on. When war did not start immediately, the unit was disbanded. They returned to Abbeville and then when the war did begin, he enlisted in the Orr's Rifles, a unit that later became part of Gen. McGowan's brigade that suffered an extremely high casualty rate. Evidently, while in training, he contracted some disease that caused his discharge and he was never again involved in an active campaign, though he must have been intensely proud of his Confederate connection for he had calling cards printed with his picture in uniform on them.

According to his 1859 diary and that of Lemuel's 1860 diary, A.E. was a very sociable person, for he recorded many instances of friends and family members' visits that included overnight stays. His father's last testament left the family farm to A.E. and his brother, John J., jointly, and in 1870, A.E. paid his brother $1,500 for his share. John executed a deed to his brother, a copy of which is included in the appendix.

Alpheus Ezekiel and Virginia Miller had one son, William Edwin.

heus Ezekiel Leslie, born Feb. 2, 1834, died March 23, 1905.   Virginia Miller Leslie, wife of Alpheus Ezekiel, born August 15, 1839, died April. 1892.

1.1.8.5 – Lewellin Luther – b. Jan, 9, 1836, d. July 29, 1836.

1.1.8.6 – John Joseph – b. May 27, 1838, d. Oct.15, 1906. He married Minta McClinton and moved to Anderson County and established a plantation. They had one child, a daughter, Daisy.

1.1.8.7 – William Edwin – b. Jan. 6, 1841, d. May 12, 1843.

The children of Thomas and Nancy Shadden Lesly

1.3.9.1 – Alexander – b. 1838.
1.3.9.2 – William – b. Sept.1839.
1.3.9.3 – Mary – b. Oct.3, 1841.
1.3.9.4 – James Wiley – b. Dec. 17, 1843.
1.3.9.5 – Thomas – b. April 17, 1845.
1.3.9.6 – John (Jack) – b. April 17, 1848.

GENERATION FIVE

(Great-great-grandchildren of Thomas and Jane Lesslie)
(Great-grandchildren of William and Ann Caldwell Lesly)
(Grandchild of James and Eliza Bird Lesly)

The children of Francis Caroline and James van Ness

1.1.2.1.1 – Elizabeth van Ness – b .1831, d. 1901.
1.1.2.1.2 – Thomas Casey van Ness – b. Feb. 15, 1847.

(Grandchildren of John Harris and Mary Gilliland Lesly)

The children of Leroy Gilliland and Indianna Childs Livingston Lesley

1.1.3.2.1 – John Thomas – b. May 12, 1835, d. July
13, 1913. He married Margaret Tucker Aug. 28, 1859,
and their union produced five children, one daughter
and five sons. John served with his father in the Seminole Indian War as a private and was soon elevated to
Lieutenant. Later during the War Between the States, he was a Captain in the Confederate Cavalry, seeing action throughout the South
and was soon raised to the rank of Major. In 1864, he was recalled
to Florida to recruit a cavalry unit to protect the state's range cattle
from Federal raiders and later to drive herds to rail heads or Confederate depots to feed the army. This unit became known as the Cow
Cavalry for their outstanding service.

The photo of the monument below was erected in Plant City,
Florida to commemorate that activity.

After the war, John served Hillsborough County as sheriff, tax assessor and tax collector, and later became Mayor. After that he was elected to the State Legislature as a Representative, and then as a State Senator. At one point he was appointed as Collector of Customs for the port of Tampa. As the city of Tampa began to grow, John realized the need for construction lumber so he built and ran a saw mill to supply that need. Among his other activities, he started a cattle business, amassing a fortune. He became one of the largest property owners in the area and sold a forty-acre tract of land to Vincent Martinez Ybor, where the cigar business was established and later became known as Ybor City.

1.1.3.2.2 – Emory Livingston – b. April 1, 1837, d. 1857.
1.1.3.2.3 – Mary Camillus – b. Oct. 4, 1845, d. 1927.

After the death of his first wife, Indianna, in 1861, Leroy married Lucy Jane Sandwich, b. April 18, 1825, d. Oct. 18, 1879. They had one child.

1.1.3.2.4 – Emma Celestia Ruth – b. Nov. 13, 1862.

The children of Theodore Josephus and Rebecca Brock Lesly

1.1.3.3.1 – Mary F. – b. March 13, 1840 died young.
1.1.3.3.2 – Margaret Ann – b. March 29, 1841.
1.1.3.3.3 – Samuel B. – b. Aug. 21, 1842.

1.1.3.3.4 – Martin Brock – b. March 20, 1844.
1.1.3.3.5 – Susan Elizabeth – b. July 21, 1845.
1.1.3.3.6 – Hannah Caroline – b. July 24, 1847.
1.1.3.3.7 – Mary E. – b. June 13, 1848.
1.1.3.3.8 – John Harris – b. Dec.25, 1850, d.1926.
1.1.3.3.9 – James A. – b. Nov. 21, 1852.
1.1.3.3.10 – William Wiley – b. April 26, 1854.
1.1.3.3.11 – Charles Henderson – b. Aug. 3, 1856.
1.1.3.3.12 – Mary Moslete – b. Nov. 3, 1859, d. 1943.
1.1.3.3.13 – Martha Lula – b. Dec. 18, 1861.

The children of James Thomas and Mary Sever Leslie

1.1.3.5.1 – Madison Livingston – b. 1844, d. 1923.
1.1.3.5.2 – Dicy Pricilla – b. 1846, d. in infancy.
1.1.3.5.3 – Moses – b. 1849, d. 1911.
1.1.3.5.4 – Lewis Gilliland – b. 1851, d. 1925.
1.1.3.5.5 – Charles – b. 1854, d. in infancy.
1.1.3.5.6 – William Sever – b. 1855, d. 1928.
1.1.3.5.7 – Mary Indianna – b. 1856, d. 1935.

The children of Frances Lesly and Andrew Sims

1.1.3.6.1 – Mary Ann Josephine Sims – b. 1835.
1.1.3.6.2 – Louise Sims – b.?
1.1.3.6.3 – Frances Pamela Sims – b.?
1.1.3.6.4 – Indianna Sims – b. Jan. 28, 1839.
1.1.3.6.5 – John Andrew Sims – b. 1841.
1.1.3.6.6 – Jefferson J. Sims – b. 1845.

(Grandchildren of Robert Hall and Elizabeth Watt Lesly)

The children of James Lewis and Eliza Wilson Leslie (note change)

1.1.5.2.1 – Eliza Lulah – b. Jan. 29, 1837.

James Lewis married, secondly, Charlotte Montague Watkins and their children were:
1.1.5.2.2 – Cornelia Ellen – b. 1846, d. Sept. 1911.
1.1.5.2.3 – Mary Lavinia – b. Dec.6, 1847, d. Dec. 17, 1914.
1.1.5.2.4 – Emma Eugenia – b. March 10, 1849, d. July 20, 1908.
1.1.5.2.5 – Annie Laurie – b. 1857, d. Oct. 17, 1862.
1.1.5.2.6 – Lewis Watkins – b. Sept. 20, 1863, d. Nov. 21, 1904.
NOTE: The sons of John Harris changed the spelling of their surnames – one to Lesley the other to Leslie and the same thing happened to the sons of Robert Hall.

The children of John Watt and Louise Jane McWhorter Lesley

1.1.5.4.1 – Anna Louise – b. Jan. 6, 1867, d. March 18, 1897.
1.1.5.4.2 – William David – b. Aug. 6, 1868, d. May 19, 1944.
1.1.5.4.3 – John Watt – b. Nov. 20, 1869, d. Nov. 16, 192_.
1.1.5.4.4 – Thomas – b. Aug. 26, 1872, d. Jan. 25, 1892.
1.1.5.4.5 – Marguerita – b. July 18, 1876, d. _____.
1.1.5.4.6 – Glenn Frazer – b. March 20, 1879, d. Nov. 1958,
1.1.5.4.7 – James Kyle – b. Aug. 19, 1882, d. Nov. 27, 1944.

(Grandchildren of William and Martha Emily White Lesly)

The children of Anna Louisa Lesly and Jesse Ward Norris

1.1.8.1.1 – Martha Lesley Norris – b. Aug. 8, 1854, d. May 20, 1926.
1.1.8.1.2 – Lucy Riah Norris – b. Dec. 9, 1857, d. Oct. 15, 1916.

The children of Virginia Elizabeth Lesly and James Archibald Montgomery

1.1.8.3.1 – William Archibald Montgomery – b. April 5, 1857, d. Sept. 27, 1924.

1.1.8.3.2 – Mary Louisa Montgomery – b. March 18, 1862, d. June 5, 1862.

1.1.8.3.3 – Elvira Virginia Montgomery – b. Sept. 22, 1866, d. young.

1.1.8.3.4 – Ella Lewis Montgomery – b. Aug. 21, 1868, d. April 21, 1934.

1.1.8.3.5 – Ernest Lesley Montgomery – b. Sept. 27, 1869, d. young.

1.1.8.3.6 – May Ola Montgomery – b. June 6, 1871, d. young.

1.1.8.3.7 – Alvin David Montgomery - b. April 2, 1874, d. 1957.

The child of Alpheus Ezekiel and Virginia Miller Lesly

1.1.8.4.1 – William Edwin – b. March 7, 1868, d. Sept. 19, 1939. He married Annie Donnald Henry Dec. 6, 1893. She was born Sept. 8, 1873, d. Dec.22, 1946. 'Will', as he was known to family and friends, grew up on the farm as did many generations of Lesly's. The farm, or a major part, remains in family posses-sion (although he stipulated in his last will and testament that the farm be sold at his wife's death with the proceeds distributed among his children).

Fortunately, two brothers, James and Mac, had the ability to pay the appraised value. The acreage was divided, and the house, with a few acres, was set aside as a third part, with James buying that portion. The house where the above children grew up, burned, and has been replaced in the exact location of the old house. The new house remains a focal point for the family and has been the site of family reunions and con-tinues to be the rallying place for family affairs.

As an only child of a family considered prosperous by the standards of the time, he would mature as an educated, cultured young man. Evidently, he considered that being an only child had certain disadvantages for he and Annie had a large family of thirteen, ten sons and three daughters, and all lived into adulthood.

This writer remembers his grandfather as a very tall man with what some would describe as a military bearing, though no records indicate he ever served in any military unit. His children remember him as a strict disciplinarian, a trait almost mandatory with so many sons, but to a grandson, he was a man of infinite wisdom and tolerance, always ready to take a child by the hand and lead him among the orchards and fields with explanations and comments. Unfortunately, there were too few years to appreciate that relationship, for he passed away in 1939, allowing only eight years of getting to know him with anything but a child's understanding.

He had a 'full head of hair', snow white in his older years, but once red and like many redheads, he had sensitive skin, which he claimed must be barber shaved. Whether the barber was actually necessary or not, he went into town every morning and not only got a shave, but also spent time talking to his friends that made the barber shop a community center.

He must have been a very gregarious individual, for he enjoyed group activities that included extended fishing trips to the Savannah River with several friends using a large tent he had made special for the purpose. He attended Clemson football games with friends and had a tennis court built in his front yard that he used extensively, and encouraged his children and their friends to use. His 650-acre farm was a breeding ground for quail, and he spent hours in the field providing succulent birds for his table, that friends helped dispose of. He was considered a 'crack' shot with his Winchester lever action rifle, and this writer's father recounted an incident where he demonstrated that ability when he shot a running animal from his front porch over 300 feet away, using one shot.

Will became a master farmer by using Clemson's out-reach programs that offered new up-to-date farming techniques and practices to those South Carolina farmers interested and willing to participate. When farming was at its peak in the 1920's, (pre boll weevil), the Leslie farm supported five tenant farming families that produced bumper crops of all commodities. One of the great joys Will experienced was sending a wagon loaded with barrels of flour, corn meal, oat meal, shelled corn, hams and other items to Thornwell Orphanage in Clinton, about 35 miles away. He considered that institution one of the finest efforts of the Presbyterian Church and felt honored to be able to provide some assistance. This was also part of his strong commitment to the church he was active in as an elder and a member of the Long Cane Society.

Will was born as William Lesly but changed the spelling to Leslie around 1911, as evidenced with the spelling of each child entered into the family Bible. He was a man of vision and enjoyed new ways of doing things like adding 'running water' to the home bathroom by building a water tank, lifting it up on a 15-foot platform and forcing water from a spring with a gasoline engine. He purchased a gas-producing engine and provided gas lighting in the home, later using the same fixtures to use the tubing for electric wires when electricity became available. Most farmers either 'ricked' their hay in the field or placed it in the barn loft with pitch forks. Will purchased a claw attached by a cable to a rail placed at the ridge of the barn, and was able to lift a wagon load of hay and drop it in the loft where needed. A team of horses was used to draw the load up to the rail and it automatically traveled down the rail until reaching the point where it was dropped.

Will Leslie enjoyed life, and while some of his joys have been mentioned, his greatest joy was his large family. He encouraged his children to return as often as possible, and those living a distance from the farm did manage many weekend visits during the summers. Since this writer was a minor fixture during the summer months, there was a chance to meet every uncle and aunt and all the cousins – one of the few, if not the only one of my generation to do so. It seems that most of those occasions saw more than one of the families there, which gave them an opportunity to assemble around the dining table, a table that would accommodate 20 diners, with Will at the head, a large ham or turkey in front of him, sharpening the carving knife with the steel, then using 'master carver' skills, loading each plate while laughing and joking with those around him.

William Edwin (Will) Leslie

Annie Henry Leslie

Though this narrative has concentrated on the males of the family and, more particularly, those males that produced descendants that extended the Leslie name, it seems appropriate at this point to include some history and antidotes about the female that shared such a large role in the family of William Edwin Leslie.

Annie Donnald Henry married Will Leslie when she was twenty years old, a city girl who learned quickly the life of a farmer's wife and raising a family. She evidently had the reputation of being a person of strong will and a mind of her own. She could probably even be described as being 'feisty' for she did not always accept conventional wisdom about things. A good demonstration of this was when a political meeting was held in the hotel meeting room in Abbeville and the well-known rule was 'males only'. The point of the meeting was of intense interest to Miss Annie, so at the time the meeting was to start, Annie went out to the buggy shed, hitched up a horse, and drove to town. When she entered the meeting room, there was a hushed gasp, but no one had the temerity to try to expel her. From that point, Miss Annie joined the meetings she wanted to with no problem.

Annie had a very strong sense of Southern culture, and she insisted her children adhere to the rules that governed. There were to be no hats worn in the house by the males, and that included Will, manners were taught early and rigidly enforced, conversation was to be civil on all occasions, and no 'nicknames' were allowed. William was never Bill, and Alpheus was always that and not Al or Alf; however that didn't apply outside, for the hands used many nicknames, but always preceded by 'Mister'.

Annie reveled in her extended family, and it seemed to this writer, she was kin to almost everyone in Abbeville. Her mother, Sarah Ellen Hill Henry, was a daughter of a large and prominent Abbeville family. She married first Andrew McIlwain who died in the war shortly after marriage. When her second husband, Francis Henry, died, she married John Calvert. Those unions were all with large Abbeville families, and the resulting number of 'cousins' was considerable, whether true kin or not.

Annie was only five feet two inches tall, but she acted like seven feet, for she ruled the household and, it seemed to this writer, that what she said was the final word on almost any subject. If how she dealt with her grandchildren was any indication of how she dealt with her children, and it is almost certain to be the case, she and Will were both strict disciplinarians. With such a large family and without exception, all turned out to be the salt of the earth type people. Discipline was not an option and the results are profound. This writer has known the sting of switches on bare legs, but the love that went along with it was obvious, for when the discipline was finished, it was finished! Miss Annie was truly a remarkable LADY.

GENERATION SIX

(Great-great-great grandchildren of Thomas and Jane Lesslie)
(Great-great grandchildren of William and Ann Caldwell Lesly)
(Great-grandchildren of William and Martha Emily White Lesly)
(Grandchildren of Alpheus Ezekiel and Virginia Miller Lesly)

The children of William Edwin and Annie Donnald Henry Leslie)

1.1.8.4.1.1 – William Edwin, Jr. – b. Jan. 10, 1895, d. Oct. 3, 1965. He married Glendel Bowen Dec. 12, 1921. She was born July 1, 1899, d. Jan. 3, 1982. William received his early education in a one-room school close to the family farm and was later tutored at home. He graduated from Clemson University and served in the U.S. Army during WW I, seeing action in France. At war's end, he returned to Abbeville and purchased a farm near his birth place.

During the depression of the 1930's, he lost the farm through questionable bank practices. As it turned out, that loss proved to be a "blessing in disguise" for he began using the engineering knowledge he received at Clemson and worked with the South Carolina State Highway Department, attaining the position of Head of Maintenance, until his retirement. At some point while employed by the Engineering Department, he was responsible for instituting the practice of painting white lines on the outside edge of the pavement surface – now considered a necessity in all fifty states. William and Glendel had two children, a son and daughter.

1.1.8.4.1.2 – Frank Henry – b. Sept. 11, 1896, d. July 17, 1985. Frank, like his older brother, received his early schooling in a one- room school house, later tutored at home, and graduated from Abbeville High School and Clemson University. He served in the U.S. Army during WW I, seeing action in France. After the war he became a teacher in the Inverness, Florida school district, then a principal and later, Superintendent. At some time in his school career he began investing in land around Inverness, later planting citrus trees. At his death, his estate amounted to several million. He married Carmen Ericson but they had no children.

1.1.8.4.1.3 – Alpheus Ezekiel – b. May 16, 1898, d. Nov. 14 1986. He married Lucy Sturdivant Dec. 28, 1924. She was born Aug. 18, 1898, died June 3, 1986. He received his schooling in a one-room school like his brothers and, like them, graduated from Clemson. Upon graduation he received a commission in the U.S. Army. He was scheduled to board a transport that would take him to France, but just hours before their departure, the Armistice was signed that ended the need for additional personnel. He was discharged and hired by AT&T, working there his entire career until retirement at age 65.

As a teenager on his father's farm, he was tasked at running the family cotton gin and learned, from necessity, to use the farm's work shop for making parts to keep the gin running during the cotton harvest. Parts could be ordered, but from out of state, and it took weeks to receive them. With the smithy, some scrap iron, and a little ingenuity, parts could be made in hours. He became so proficient in the shop that he made a wood lathe using scrap iron, parts from discarded equipment, and worn-out files and rasps for the turning tools. That lathe is being used by his son and namesake at the time of this writing – almost 100 years after it was made. True to his heritage he became a ruling elder in the Presbyterian Church, and after serving many years on the session, was named an elder emeritus. Alpheus and Lucy had four children, three sons and one daughter.

1.1.8.4.1.4 – Albert Henry – b. May 16, 1898, d. Dec.28, 1978. He married Sydelle Graves of Abbeville April 11, 1923. She was born Aug. 4, 1901, died Aug. 4 1991. He, like his twin brother, Alpheus, attended a one-room school for early years, tutored at home until he entered Clemson University, and then returned to help his father where he operated the cotton gin among other duties. He was hired by the Atlantic Coast Railroad as an Electrical Engineer and transferred to Florida where he remained for the rest of his life, retiring in Jacksonville. Albert and Sydelle had three daughters.

1.1.8.4.1.5 – David Hill – b. June 29, 1900, d. July 7, 1971. He married Thelma Hagen in 1934. David moved to New Port News, Virginia, and worked in the shipyards until WW II when he enlisted in the Navy. At war's end, he returned to the shipyards until retirement. He and Thelma had five children.

1.1.8.4.1.6 – Virginia Miller – b. Aug. 7, 1902, d. April 26, 1988. She graduated from Abbeville High School and Winthrop College, and then became a home economics teacher in Florida, later to become Florida State Superintendent for the Home Economics Department. After retirement she returned to the Abbeville area and lived in a retirement center at Due West. She was unmarried.

1.1.8.4.1.7 – John Donnald – b. Oct. 18, 1904, d. Sept. 1, 1951. He graduated from Abbeville High School and attended a trade school where he became an electrical engineer. He married Georgia Philbert in 1938, and began working at the Oakridge Atomic Center in Tennessee, where he died of unexplained causes. John and Georgia had two children, a son and a daughter.

1.1.8.4.1.8 – Sarah Ellen – b. Sept. 14, 1906, d. ? Sarah graduated from Abbeville High School and Winthrop College and, after graduation, taught school in North Carolina. She married Rudolph Thunberg of Sweden, who was Assistant Postmaster of Fort Bragg, on June 24, 1929. They made their home in Fayetteville, N.C. and had two children, a son and a daughter.

1.1.8.4.1.9 – Robert Hall – b. Feb. 3, 1909, d. May 9, 1986. He graduated from Abbeville High School and married Dorothy Nickles of Hodges, S.C. She was born Jan. 6,

1912, died Aug. 27, 2003. Robert operated a dairy at Ware Shoals, S.C. for several years. When his brother, Mac, who was in charge of managing the family farm, returned to the U.S. Navy at the start of WW II, Robert returned home to take Mac's place. He continued a dairy operation there as well as general farming, growing corn, wheat, oats, sugar cane hay and continued raising sheep, swine and the necessary horses and mules. At his mother's death, the farm was sold as per his father's instructions, and he worked for a feed distributor until his retirement. Robert and Dorothy had four children, three sons and one daughter.

1.1.8.4.1.10 – Mac Henry – b. Feb. 1, 1911, d. June 9, 1979. He graduated from Abbeville High School and afterwards worked with his father on the family farm until he joined the U.S. Navy. After serving 12 years, Mac returned to the farm at his father's death and was in charge of it until WW II started. He then returned to the Navy until war's end and, after discharge, returned to the farm. At his mother's death, he and his brother, James, paid the appraised value of the farm and divided the 600 acres between them. Mac was known throughout the local area for the hash and sausage he produced. He was one of the first to use metal cans to preserve the hash, and was prospering until the federal Government decreed that his operation did not meet government standards, and he was forced to cease selling to the public, though he continued his hash production for his and the family's use for several years. Mac married Francis Botts but they had no children.

1.1.8.4.1.11 – James Lewis – b. March 4, 1913, d. April 24, 2003. He graduated from Abbeville High School where he participated in several sports including football. Soon after graduation, he joined the CCC and was sent to Oregon. The Civilian Conservation Corps was responsible for projects such as roads, wildlife refuge facilities construction, and many other civic/community improvement projects as a result of the depression of the 1930's. After his CCC days, he returned to work with his father on the family farm until he was offered a job at the local mill. In November, 1939, he married Martha Wilson and continued living at the 'home place'. He later was hired by the Seaboard Railroad on a part-time basis and soon became fulltime, but the schedule allowed him to continue working the land he loved so much. He retired after 37 years of railroad work and then began growing beef cattle in an effort to utilize his acreage. James loved to talk about his family history and especially enjoyed planning and hosting family reunions. James and Martha had three children, two sons and a daughter.

1.1.8.4.1.12 – Nickolas Miller – b. Aug. 13, 1915, d. Dec. 22, 1989. He graduated from Abbeville High School, attended a business college in Jacksonville, and after graduation, entered business there. He enlisted in the Army at the start of WW II, seeing action in Europe. Upon discharge he returned to Jacksonville and continued his business career. He married Mary Edwards Aug. 5, 1975. Nickolas and Mary had two children, a son and a daughter.

1.1.8.4.1.13 – Annie Donnald – b. May 10, 1918, d. Jan. 20 2003. She graduated from Abbeville High School and attended a business college in Atlanta, Georgia, where she resided with her brother, Alpheus. She later moved to Atlanta and worked for Spalding Sporting Goods. When WW II started, she enlisted in the Army and served in the motion picture service. On November 17, 1946, she married Uriah Corkrum from Walla Walla, Wash. They made their home in Walla Walla where Uriah began farming on a large scale, specializing in crops such as English peas. Uriah and Annie Donnald had three children, two sons and a daughter.

GENERATION SEVEN

(Great-great-great-great grandchildren of Thomas and Jane Lesslie)
(Great-great-great grandchildren of William and Ann Caldwell Lesly)
(Great-great grandchildren of William and Martha Emily White Lesly)
(Great-grandchildren of Alpheus Ezekiel and Virginia Miller Leslie)
(Grandchildren of William Edwin and Annie Henry Leslie)

The children of William Edwin, Jr. and Glendel Leslie

1.1.8.4.1.1.1 – William Edwin II – b. April 4, 1923, d. July 18, 1996. He graduated from Union High School and entered the U.S. Army. Upon discharge he worked in the Mill, retiring at age 65, remaining in Union until his death.

1.1.8.4.1.1.2 – Marcellene (Mac) – b. Sept. 7, 1929. Graduated from Union, South Carolina High School and Erskine College. She married William (Red) Myers and they are the parents of five children. She taught primary school for several years after her marriage. Now Mac makes her home in Greenwood, South Carolina.

The children of Alpheus Ezekiel and Lucy Sturdivant Leslie

1.1.8.4.1.3.1 – Robert Edward (Ed) – b. Oct. 3, 1926, d. March 23, 2007. Ed graduated from Decatur Boys High School, Decatur, Georgia, and attended Emory University briefly. He joined the Navy and became a pilot, and at war's end continued flying as a reserve until eye problems forced his retirement. He graduated from the University of Georgia after regular Naval duty and entered business as a stock broker, from which he retired. He married Jane Moore of Griffin, Georgia, and they had one daughter.

1.1.8.4.1.3.2 – Alpheus Ezekiel, Jr. – b. Oct. 10, 1927.
Al is known to family as 'Bubba'. He graduated from Decatur Boy's High School and entered Georgia Tech in a special U.S. Navy training program. At the end of WW II, he
entered the University of Georgia and graduated shortly
after his brother, Ed. He entered business, finally working for Kraft
Foods until retirement. He learned woodworking, partly from his father,
but primarily by working hard at the craft, and has attained unofficially
'master craftsman' status. He married Kathryn Greer who died March
29, 1991, but had no children. He married Lafern Mauk Jones December 4, 1993.

1.1.8.4.1.3.3 – Donald William – b. April 18, 1931.
Graduated from Decatur Boy's High School and attended
Presbyterian College, Clinton, South Carolina, until called
to active duty during the Korean War in the U.S. Navy.
Upon discharge he graduated from Georgia State Univer-
sity. He worked in the textile business for several years and then entered
real estate, becoming a general contractor, specializing in home construction. Don married Marian Henderson March 16, 1957, and they
have three children, two sons and one daughter.

1.1.8.4.1.3.4 – Mary Sturdivant – b. March 29, 1934.
Mary graduated from Decatur Girl's High School, Decatur, Georgia, and Erskine College. After graduating,
Mary married a fellow Erskine grad, James Williams, who
became a renowned Methodist minister. Mary learned to
play the piano at an early age and progressed to the pipe organ, serving
as the Church organist where her husband preached. She has continued
her organ and piano functions wherever called on. Mary and Jimmy are
the parents of four daughters.

The children of Albert Henry and Sidelle Graves

1.1.8.4.1.4.1 – Jean Ellen – b. Feb.1924, d. December 30, 1994.
Jean graduated from Lee High School, Jacksonville, and Florida State

University. She then worked as a librarian at the University of Florida and later taught school. She became an accomplished artist specializing in portrait painting. She married Harold Winters and they had two children, a son and a daughter.

1.1.8.4.1.4.2 – Margaret Sydelle – b. May 4, 1926, d. April 21, 2004. She graduated from Lee High School, Jacksonville, and Florida State University. She entered public service work and then moved to San Francisco where she taught school. She met Frank (Dutch) Meyers there and they were later married and moved to North Carolina. Margaret and Dutch had three children, two sons and a daughter.

1.1.8.4.1.4.3 – Ann Henry – b. June 23, 1932. Ann graduated from Landon High School, Jacksonville, and the University of Florida. She taught elementary school for many years. She raises, trains and shows dogs professionally and participated with her husband in historic reenactments. She married George Maust and they have four children.

The children of David Hill and Thelma Hagen Leslie

1.1.8.4.1.5.1 – Nicholas Miller – b. March 1936, d. 1987.

1.1.8.4.1.5.2 – Harper – b. Nov.1 1937, d. April 15, 1968.

1.1.8.4.1.5.3 – Gene Awtry – b. 1940.

1.1.8.4.1.5.4 – William Edwin – b. June 16, 1943.

The children of John Donnald and Georgia Philbert Leslie

1.1.8.4.1.7.1 – Donnald Philbert – b. March 1939. He graduated from Carlisle Military Academy, Bamberg, South Carolina, and attended The Citadel, later entering business as a stockbroker. Donnald now lives in South Africa.

1.1.8.4.1.7.2 – Margaret Ann (Peggy) – b. April 26, 1940. She graduated from Union High School and Erskine College with a music major and taught music. She is an accomplished organist as well as pianist. Peggy became a specialist in behavioral education and married George Amos Pierce, Jr. Peggy and George have three daughters.

The children of Rudolph S.A. and Sarah Ellen Leslie Thunberg

1.1.8.4.1.8.1 – Ann Leslie Thunberg – b. July 3, 1936. Ann graduated from Fayetteville High School and Women's College of North Carolina with a degree in music. She taught piano for many years. Ann married Wayne Yelverton and they have no children.

1.1.8.4.1.8.2 – Rudolf Thunberg – b. April 26, 1938. Rudolf graduated from Fayetteville High School and Duke University, and then received a graduate degree from Princeton. He worked for the Federal Reserve of N.Y and later formed his own consulting firm. He married Debra Jamroz and they have one daughter.

The children of Robert Hall and Dorothy Nickles Leslie

1.1.8.4.1.9.1 – Robert Hall Jr., (Bobby) – b. Feb.6, 1938. Bobby graduated from Greenwood, South Carolina High School, worked for S.E. Machine Works, then Monsanto until retirement. His hobby was flying light planes as well as instructing pilots of same. He married Carolyn Bell and they have three children.

1.1.8.4.1.9.2 – Charles Edward – b. Dec. 11, 1940. He graduated from Greenwood High School and attended the University of South Carolina. Charles worked for Greenwood Mills until retirement. He married Christy Goodenough with whom he has two children. They divorced and he is now married to Earlene Thompson. They live on Lake Greenwood and enjoy boating, fishing, shag dancing, and spending time with grandchildren.

1.1.8.4.1.9.3 – William Benton – b. Dec. 11, 1944, d. Sept. 1995. He graduated from Greenwood High School and Lander College and served in the U.S. Air Force. William worked for the South Carolina Rehabilitation Department as a counselor until a fatal heart attack. He loved shrimping, fishing and boiled peanuts. He was married but had no children.

1.1.8.4.1.9.4 – Mary Louise – b. Dec. 20, 1946. She graduated from Greenwood High School, worked for Greenwood County in Clerk of Court's office and then as the Clerk of Court. Like her mother, she is a great cook and a devoted grandmother, enjoying time with all grandchildren, especially in their swimming pool. She married Benny Davis and they have two daughters.

The children of James Lewis and Martha Wilson Leslie

1.1.8.4.1.11.1 – James Lewis (Jimmy) – b. March 26, 1942. He graduated from Abbeville High School and Clemson University,  and then served in the U.S. Coast Guard. Jimmy returned to graduate school at the University of South Carolina and graduated with a Doctor of Jurisprudence Degree. He owns Windward Point Yacht Club on Lake Murray. He married Gertrude Denise Fox and has a daughter.

1.1.8.4.1.11.2 – Marie Ann – (Ann) b. April 2, 1945.
Ann graduated from Abbeville High School then Winthrop
College, majoring in Home Economics. After graduation
she married her high school love, Franklin Pursley in 1967.
While living in Indiana, she earned a Master's in Education
from Purdue University and she taught in various capacities and locations as her husband's railroad employment moved them around. Every
vacation was a trip home to her beloved Abbeville and the farm she grew
up on. As her parents aged, she spent more time there in caring for
them. After their deaths, she and Franklin remodeled her parents' home
as they intended to continue living there, at least on a part time basis.
Her parents, in their gracious hospitality, always made their home available to the large Leslie family as a welcome place to visit, and the long
habit of returning to the 'old home place' continued by most of the
family. Ann and Franklin intend to continue that practice and have
made provisions to retain the farm for the indefinite future. Franklin
and Ann have two daughters.

1.1.8.4.1.11.3 – Henry Stephen (Steve) – b. Sept. 20, 1950. He
graduated from Abbeville High School where he participated
in band, 4H and football. He graduated from Clemson University and, after a short time in the textile industry, became
involved in the insurance business. Steve now owns an insurance and financial planning business. He married Connie Price and
they have four children. Steve and Connie divorced and Steve is now
married to Thelma "Elle".

The children of Nicholas Miller and Mary Edwards Leslie

1.1.8.4.1.12.1 – Nickolas Miller, Jr. – b. May 15,
1949. He graduated from Wolfson High School, Jacksonville and Florida State University. Nickolas is an outstanding banjo musician in blue grass bands.

1.1.8.4.1.12.2 – Robin Anne – b. May 8. She graduated from Wolfson High School, Jacksonville and the University of South Carolina.

Robin Anne earned a Master of Education degree from the University of North Florida. She married Thomas Copeland and they have one daughter. That marriage ended and she is now married to Everitt Malcolm. They make their home at Jacksonville Beach.

The children of Uriah Franklin and Annie Donnald Leslie Corkrum

1.1.8.4.1.13.1 – Virginia Ann – b. June 22, 1948. Virginia Ann graduated from Walla Walla High School and Washington State University, and Teachers College in Atlanta, Georgia. She then taught elementary school and married Roger Hope. She and Roger have eight children.

1.1.8.4.1.13.2 – Uriah Franklin (Franklin), Jr. – b. Dec. 13, 1949. Franklin graduated from Walla Walla High School and Washington State University. Franklin pursued a career in advertising and is an avid snow skier. He married Kay Johnson and they have two children.

1.1.8.4.1.13.3 – Marion Barlow (Barlow) – b. Aug. 9, 1953. Barlow graduated from Walla Walla High School and the University of South Carolina. He enjoyed a long career in real estate. He married Dalia.

This is not the end of the chronicle of this family, for there is an eighth and ninth generation that exists, and it is obvious that a tenth will soon be started. Significant information has been collected about these generations, however, their inclusion must be postponed until a later time when other people are available and, hopefully, interested enough to record them in a Volume Two. The collected data will be included in this volume for the assistance for those who will follow.

FAMILY REUNIONS

1926 – The first recorded reunion and probably the first of any kind for this family. Present were twelve of the thirteen children (David missing), four spouses and four grandchildren. Six of the thirteen were still at home. (Sarah was away at college and home for the summer.) Four of the children were in Florida (Frank, Alpheus, Albert and Virginia), one in South Carolina (William), one in Virginia – the missing David, and it is not known where John was living at the time.

From l to r: 1st row – Robert, James, Annie Donnald (slightly behind), Nickolas and Mac, *2nd row* – William holding Billy, Virginia, Will, Annie, Sarah and John. *3rd row* – Glendel, Sydelle holding Margaret, Albert holding Jean, Lucy, Alpheus holding Ed, Carmen and Frank.

Will inherited a one story cottage-style house that easily accommodated the family as he grew up but enlarged it into a two story as his family grew. One of the things he made sure to include in the new structure was a dining room that would hold a large table. When the enlargement was completed, Will purchased a mahogany table with ten leaves that would seat twenty people comfortably and, on occasion, twenty-two. When several of his children and their spouses managed to be at the 'home place' for the same weekend, Will enjoyed his place at the end of the table with an opportunity to show off his 'master carving' skills with jokes and great deal of laughter all around the table. A truly happy family!

1956 Reunion – Thirty years since the first, and again, twelve children present (John died in 1951), ten spouses, twenty grandchildren and two great-grandchildren. William Edwin (Will) died in 1939 and

L to R 1st row: Louise Leslie, Ann Leslie, Robin Leslie, Steve Leslie, Dub Myers, Nicky Leslie, Hal Winters; *2nd row:* Billy Leslie, Nicky Leslie, Benton Leslie, Charles Leslie, Harper Leslie, Bobby Leslie, Jimmy Leslie; *3rd row:* Marcellene holding Sissy, William, Peggy, Virginia, Nickolas, Mary, Dorothy, Robert; *4th row:* Glendel, Donnie, Annie Donnald, Jimmy Williams, Mary Williams, Lucy, Alpheus, Donald; *5th row:* James, Martha, Carmen, Frank, Sydelle, Albert, Jean Winters, Harold Winters; *6th row:* Sarah, Rudolph, Mac, Francis, Thelma, David.

Annie in 1946, and during their lifetimes, most of (maybe all) of the children returned for weekend visits and some for entire weeks. Both Will and Annie reveled in their large family and encouraged as many of the visits as possible.

1960 Reunion – Twelve children, nine spouses, 16 grandchildren, 6 great- grandchildren. James and Martha enjoyed having so many at the 1956 reunion they decided to hold another only four years later – and another great turnout. A sure sign that this family truly enjoyed each other's company.

1978 Reunion – 80 in attendance. They came from Washington State, New York, Texas, Florida, and most states in between. See how a family grows. Counting all of the cousins and their children has proven to be an impossible task so the numbers will be left to your imagination. Everyone did have a great time, though, renewing the family connections.

1989 Reunion – about 86 attendees.

1999 Reunion – about 90 attendees. Held on July 4th and boy, was it hot! You can see everybody squinting in the group picture but everyone still enjoyed getting back together. Only two of the original thirteen were able to get back to the 'ole home place' – Annie Donnald came all the way from Washington State and James only had to go out the front door.

2012 Reunion – Somebody got smart and had the group picture taken under the 500-year-old oak trees – what a difference from the 1999 reunion. The oldest attendee was Alpheus Ezekiel Leslie at 85 (namesake of his great grandfather), and the youngest was Catherine Hanna – two months old. A special guest seen on the front row was Dr. Lowery Ware, local historian, special friend, and native of Abbeville County.

As much pleasure as James and Martha had in hosting these re-unions over the years, it seems a shame they could not be with us. James died in 2008 at 95, and Martha a year later. How proud they would have been of the great job their children did filling in for them.

PICTURES OF FAMILY INTEREST

Below is the house that Will built for his and Annie's growing family that would eventually become thirteen children. He enlarged a one story cottage-style house in the early 1900's. Construction was underway while William, the oldest son, was a student at Clemson University. A letter exists from William to his mother inquiring about the progress and wondering when it would be finished. Most of the lumber used in the enlargement project was cut and processed on the farm this house rests on. Note the steps with no hand rail. The picture on the next page shows that a metal hand rail was added. The original house had wooden steps but this picture shows that they were replaced with concrete.

The old house in winter

The old house in summer

What was left after a 1971 cold and stormy night of high winds, large fires in the fireplaces, and old, dry mortar in a chimney. A spark escaped through the bricks of one of the chimneys and the winds found a tiny place to enter the attic, and the race was on to get as much out of the house as possible. James and Martha made a heroic effort to drag out many antiques and valuables before the flames made it too dangerous for further salvage attempts. An old roll top desk in the sitting room to the left of the entrée hall that held many of the financial records relating to the years of farming, real estate transactions and historical interests, was too heavy for two people to move and was consumed in the fire. The attic was full of memorabilia of all kinds from almost two centuries of living at the same place, though not the same house, but that is where the fire was the hottest and all was lost. Fortunately, Nickolas visited a year or so before the catastrophic event and rescued some of the historic material, including a diary written by his grandfather that would later be transcribed and printed by a nephew.

The new house, built on the exact site of the old one, uses many of the bricks that were salvaged. This house does not have the twelve foot ceilings as the old one did, but does have many modern conveniences including an up-to-date heating system, modern baths, and kitchens the old house lacked. Since James and Martha passed away, their children have modernized it even further.

The dinner bell in the front is the original that was used to call the 'hands' to the mid-day meal and mark the end of the work day. Every farm in the area had one of these 'communication' devices. Watches were too expensive to own, and usually a messenger would have to visit two or more different fields to accomplish what the one bell could.

A hitching post was also rescued from the old environment as a memento just as the bell is used. There is a rich history of successful farming for over two hundred years at this farm, and every effort has been made to acknowledge and venerate the ancestors who toiled and struggled to create an entity that is available for those of today to enjoy.

From L to R: 1st row – Mac, Nickolas and Robert; 2nd row – William, Virginia, Annie Donnald, Sarah and James; 3rd row – Frank, Alpheus, Albert and David.

All twelve of the living children of William Edwin and Annie Donnald Henry Leslie as they looked thirty years after the first reunion of 1926, assembled on the steps of the old house they grew up in. It may sound prejudiced but this is truly a fine group of people – all living lives that reflected their heritage of discipline and Christian instruction. Real salt of the earth people!

L to R: 1st row – Sarah, Annie Donnald and Robert; 2nd row – Mac, Virginia, James and Alpheus; 3rd row – Nickolas, Mary Starke Davis, a cousin, Glendel, widow of William, and Frank. Mary Starke Davis was the last owner of the Burt-Starke House who willed the house and furnishings to the Abbeville Historical Society.

The living children of William Edwin and Annie Donnald Henry Leslie, plus the spouse of one of the sons and a cousin, assembled as a group for the last time in 1978, on the steps of the new house.

Robert and Dorothy
Leslie

Red and
Marcellene Myers

James and Martha
Leslie

Albert and Sydelle Leslie

Alpheus and Lucy at their
Sixtieth Wedding Anniversary

A young Martha & James Leslie

Annie holding Sarah & David

George Maust

Old Tenant House

Don & Ann

James at Cane Mill

Don & Caroline

Martha & Lynn
with cookbook

Scene at 1956 Reunion

The old two-seater

Old barn & dairy shed

1956 – Steve on steps, Lucy Janie & Martha

1956 Reunion Scene

Edgewood one-room school

Brothers and sisters at the Sixtieth Wedding Anniversary of Alpheus and Lucy.
L to R: Alpheus, Virginia, Robert, Sarah, James.

Annie Donnald & grandchildren in kitchen

Newest family member –
Catherine Hanna –
What A Doll!

Cowboy Steve in the Jonquils

Wm. E. as a
young boy

Christmas
in old
house –
Franklin

Drew, Mary and Pamela Leslie

Recognition of Colonial Origins

Welcome Leslies
And all your folks, to a Bonnie Reunion
At Leslie Oaks!

2012 Welcome Sign

Alpheus's Folks

Chief Ian, son Alexander, James, Annie D.,
Sarah, Nickolas, Martha & Jimmy

A bunch of the boys:
Todd, Daniel, Jimmy, Franklin

Nickolas's Crew

Ranelagh & Piper

Elle and Steve Leslie

Peggy, Leslie, Gus, & Patty

Alison & daughter Catherine
with Jimmy & Jennifer
looking on.

Martha Leslie

James getting a toast on his birthday, Bubba, and Don

Jane & Marian hula-hooping

Fern & Franklin on scooter

Family of Alpheus & Lucy

Annie Donald & family

Carol Lynn, Grayson and Caroline

Dorothy Leslie & children

George & Ann Maust with children

James & Martha Leslie & family

Earlene
& Charles

Don & Marian

Brothers & Cousins

SUPPORTING DOCUMENTS FOR CHRONICLE OF A SCOTCH-IRISH FAMILY

1. Colonial Council Meeting Minutes of Dec. 4, 1765. This document lists the people that have "recently arrived from Great Briton & Belfast in Ireland", evidently on the Prince of Wales, (though it does not list the name of the ship). The list includes names and ages and normally the ages are in sequential order but the names of Wm. Lesslie and what looks like either Bart or Mart out of order – Wm – 8, Mart 11.
2. The abstract of "Petitions for Land from the S.C. Council Journals" by Brent Holcomb indicates the ages of Wm. and Mart are recorded differently in the British copy.
3. British version of the Dec. 4, 1765 Council minutes show that Wm.'s age as 11 as the family Bible indicates and his sibling as not Mart or Bart but Margaret as 8. Since both Thomas and Jane are listed as 40 and John and Mary at 38 it is assumed that Thomas and Jane are husband and wife and John and Mary are.
4. Page from the Leslie Family Bible shows William Lesly's birth date as Nov. 10, 1754 – making his age in 1765 as 11.
5. Recorded survey of 400 acre land grant awarded to Thomas Lesslie. The award issued by the Council states that the acreage is to be in Boonesboro Township but the survey states the acreage is 'near' the township. Computer programs designed to locate land grants on modern maps show Thomas's grant adjacent to the city of Abbeville which is several miles south of the township.
6. Survey dated 1822 of present Leslie farm begun in 1773.
7. South Carolina state reaffirmation of Colonial grant. No copy of grant has been found but other data indicate a grant was issued to Thomas Lesly in 1773.
8. Last Will and Testament of William Lesly passing title to the farm to his son William.

9. Last Will and Testament of William to sons Alpheus E. and John J. Lesly.

10. Buyout agreement between brothers John J. and Alpheus E. Lesly showing John J. selling his half interest in the farm to his brother.

11. Last Will and Testament of William Edwin leaving the farm to his wife with instructions to sell the farm and distribute the proceeds equally among their children at her death.

12. Affidavit from Thomas Lesly, son of Thomas Lesslie relating experience as a member of militia unit during Revolutionary War and stating that he was born in County Antrim, Northern Ireland and that his militia unit rendezvoused at his fathers' farm.

13. Affidavit from James Thomas Leslie claiming a pension earned from service in the Seminole Indian War and explaining that he changed the spelling of his Surname in the interim.

14. Copy of a hand written sales contract by David Lesly for his house and ninety five acres to Nickolas Miller. The house referred to was later purchased by John L. Hill and is known as "The Hill House", presently owned by Billy and Linda Hill. The significant issue of this document is that Nickolas Miller later became this writer's great great-grandfather for his daughter, Virginia, married Alpheus E. Lesly. Additionally, another daughter, Mary, married James Starke who bought and restored the second house David Lesly built and is now known as the Burt-Starke House. The Starke daughters, Mary and Fanny, were considered cousins by the Leslie family.

Read also the following Petitions praying for the Town Allowed by the said Act: viz.

James Gray 33
Martha Walker 15
Thomas Walker 7
John Walker 14
Samuel Walker 12

THE Petitioners produced proper Certificates of their good behaviour but it appearing they had not paid for their passages ORDERED that the Certificates be delivered to Mess.rs Torrant Pouag & Co. as above.

Read also the following Petitions praying for the County allowed by the said Act

... Leslie Aged	40 Years	John Webb	24 Years
... Leslie	13	Barbara ...	2
W.m Leslie	9	Anne Crossley	15
Ma.. Leslie	11	Susannah Crossley	7
Thomas Leslie	6	Catherine Moore	33
Jane Leslie	9	Anne Moore	12
Mary Leslie	30	Hugh Moore	13
W.m Leslie	13	James Moore	10
... Leslie	11	William Moore	2
Samuel Leslie	7	...nnel Walker	30
John Leslie	4	Jane Maxwell	26

PETITIONS FOR LAND FROM SOUTH CAROLINA COUNCIL JOURNALS

[Meeting of Wednesday 4 December 1765]

Read also the following petitions praying for the Bounty allowed by the said Act

Jane Lesslie	40		Catherine Moore	33
Ann Leslie	13		Ann Moore	14
Wm Lesslie	8 [11]*		Hugh Moore	13 [10]*
Mar't Lesslie	11 [8]*		James Moore	10 [13]*
Thomas Lesslie	5		William Moore	2
Jane Lesslie	2		Jannet Walker	38
Mary Lesslie	38		Jane Maxwell	28
Wm Lesslie	13		Rob't Maxwell	12
Jane Lesslie	11		Alexd'r Maxwell	10
Samuel Lesslie	7		John Maxwell	8
John Lesslie	4		Nicholas Maxwell	5
Eliz'h Webb	30		Mary Webb	14
Andrew Webb	10		Sarah Webb	6
John Webb	2		Sarah McClue	26* [McCue]
Barbara McClue	2**		Martha Crossley	30
Anne Crossley	15		Mary Crossley	9
Susannah Crossley	7		Bridget McCormack	20

Martha Mathers	aged 18 years	100 acres
Sarah Lacey	aged 18 years	100 acres
John Black	aged 16	100 acres
Andrew Beryhill	aged 18	100 acres

The Petitioners Severally produceing Certificates of their being Protestants & also of their good behaviour & receipts for their passages, Ordered that the Clerk do grant them Certificates to the Public Treasurer to pay them the several Bounties allowed by the said Act.

Read also the petitions of the following Protestants lately arrived from Great Britain praying for Warrants of Survey & the Bounty viz

Donald Harper	100)	In Boonesborough or
James Gaillard	100)	Belfast Township
Lawrence Hutchins	350)	In or near Orangeburgh Township
Samuel Kingwood	200)	

Ordered that the Secretary do prepare Warrants of Survey & that the Clerk do grant Certificates to the Public Treasurer, to pay them Bounty as prayed for by the petitions.
'Variations in the British copy.
**The name in the British copy is Barnaba McCue

PETITIONS FOR LAND FROM SOUTH CAROLINA COUNCIL JOURNAL:

<u>[Meeting of Wednesday 4 December 1765]</u>

Read also the following Petitions praying for the Bounty Viz

Sarah Hutchins	38 years
Alice Hutchins	7
Martha Kingwood	40
Rich'd Walter Hutchins	11
Mary Hutchins	4
Jacob Kingwood	11

And they producing proper Certificates & receipts for their Passages, Ordered that the Clerk do grant them Certificates to the Public Treasurer agreeable to the directions of the said Act.

<u>Meeting of Monday 9 December 1765</u>

Pages 677-678: His Honor the Lieutenant Governor also informed the Board that some of the Irish people who lately arrived in this province on the Bounty and whose orders for the same had been made payable to Messrs. Torrans, Pouag & Co in consideration for their passages had been with him and set forth that they apprehended they were entitled the twenty shillings sterling provided by the said Act for to buy them tools and Mn Pouag attending was called in and produced an assignment for their Bounty generally value received by them in their passage to this place. The Board upon recourse had to the Act were of opinion that they were not authorized under it to give orders in consideration of their passages for more than the four pounds sterling and as the assignment was a matter proper for a private litigation it was out of their province to meddle with it.

FAMILY RECORD.

BIRTHS.	BIRTHS.
Wm Leely born 10 of Nov 1754 & died Dec 30 1821.	Thomas Leslie born June 16th 1775 Died 14th April 1827.
Ann Caldwell born Sept 29 1759 & died July 25th 1800.	David Leslie born June 15 1799 Died Feb 9th 1844.
Wm Leely & Ann Caldwell Married April 9th 1778.	Ezekiel Leslie born 1st March 1791 Died 2^d of Oct 1809
Thomas Leely born May 12 1780 & died July 3. 1784	Samuel Watt Leslie born Sep^t 1. 1803 Died ___
James born Aug 6th 1782 & died August 9. 1806	
John Harris Leely born 11th of Feb 1784. Died ___	Martha Leslie Norris born May 17. 1854
Jane Leely born 1st Feb 1786 Died 2^d of Aug 1807.	Lucie Rieth Norris born Dec 9th 1856.
Robert Hall Leslie born Sept 14. 1787. Died April 9th 1847.	William A Montgomery born April 5 1859.
Elizabeth Leely born Dec 1. 1889 & died 19 Aug 1807.	William Edwin Leely born May 7th 1868.
Ann Leely born Nov 9 1891 died ___	Annie Donald Henry born Sep 7th 1873.
Wm Leely born April 25 1718 Died Feb 9 1861)	

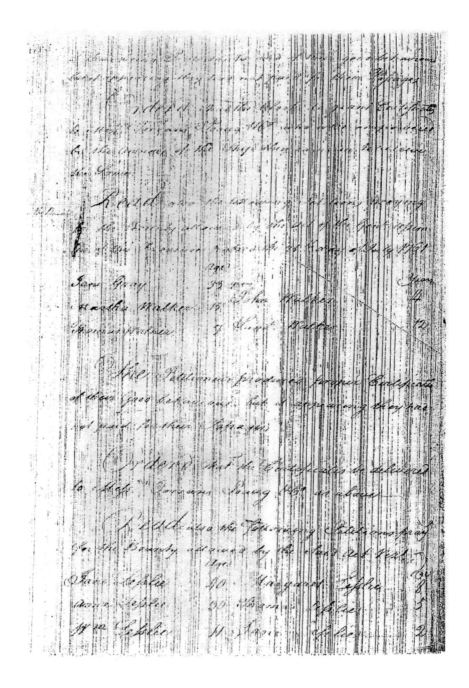

South Carolina Archives & History - View Image

S213184: Colonial Plat Books (Copy Series)

LESSLIE, THOMAS, PLAT FOR 400 ACRES ON LONG CANE CREEK.

| Return to image index |

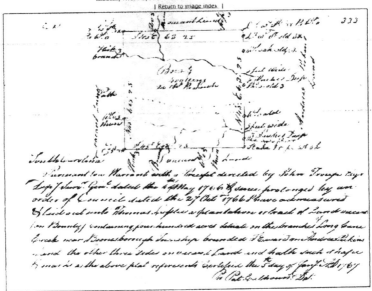

| Return to image index |

THE STATE OF SOUTH-CAROLINA.

To all to whom these Presents shall come,
Greeting:

Know ye, *That in pursuance of an Act of the Legislature, entitled "An Act for establishing the mode of granting the Lands now vacant in this State, and for allowing a compensation to be received for some Lands that have been granted; passed the 19th day of February, 1791;* We have Granted *and by these Presents do Grant unto* William Lesly

His Heirs and Assigns, a Plantation or Tract of Land, containing *six hundred & fifty acres (Surveyed for him the 8th August 18.. situate in Abbeville District, on Calhoun Creek, Waters of Little River*

having such shape, form and marks as are represented by a Plat hereunto annexed, together with all ... woods, waters, water courses, profits, commodities, appurtenances and hereditaments whatsoever, thereunto lying. To have and to Hold *the said Tract of Six Hundred and Fifty*

Acres of ... and singular other the premises hereby granted unto the said William Lesly *his Heirs and Assigns, forever ...*

GIVEN UNDER THE SEAL OF THE STATE.

Witness, *His Excellency* ... *Governor and Commander ... in and over the said State, at Columbia, this ... day of ... Anno Domini, one thousand eight hundred and twenty ... and in the forty... Year of the Independence of the United States of America.*

116

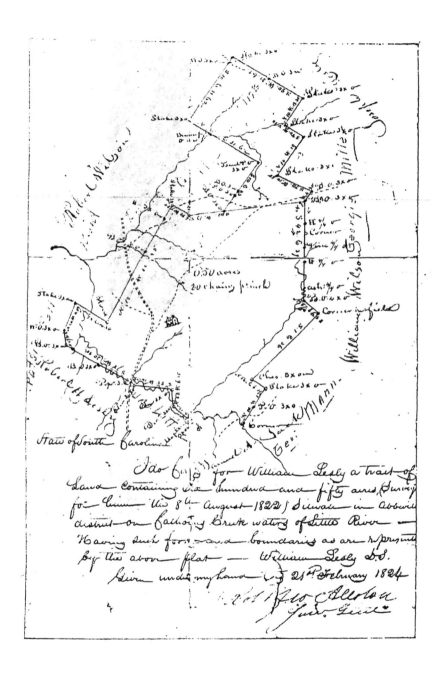

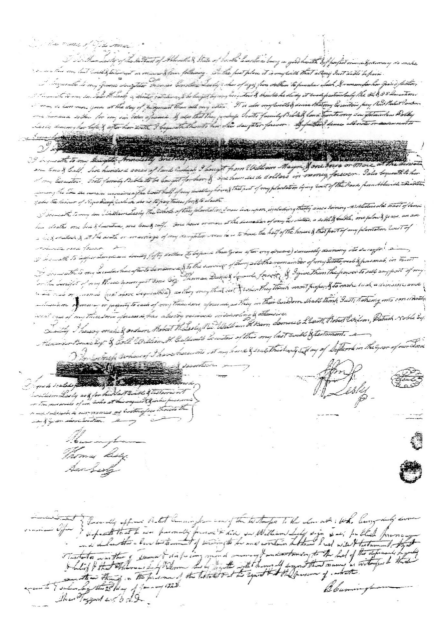

I William Lesly of the District of Abbeville and State of South Carolina being of sound mind and memory and considering the uncertainty of life do make ordain publish and declare this to be my last will and testament: That is to say after all my lawful debts are paid and discharged the residue of my estate real and personal I give bequeath and dispose of as follows: To wit:

I give my plantation on which I now reside bounded by lands of James Gordon William Newel Samuel Reid J W Lesly & others to my sons A. E. & J J Lesly

I give my plantation tools and implements household and kitchen furniture together with the stock of horses cattle sheep hogs &c of which I am or may be possessed to my sons A E & J J Lesly

And I hereby nominate constitute and appoint my sons Adams E & J J Lesly Executors of this my last will and testament In witness whereof I have hereunto subscribed my name and affixed my seal This the second day of August eighteen hundred and sixty five

At the request of the Testator and in his } Wm Lesly [L.S.]
presence and in the presence of each other we }
have hereunto subscribed our names as }
witnesses of the signing and sealing }
of the foregoing instrument }

Test, Samuel Reid
Test, T. H. Reid.

119

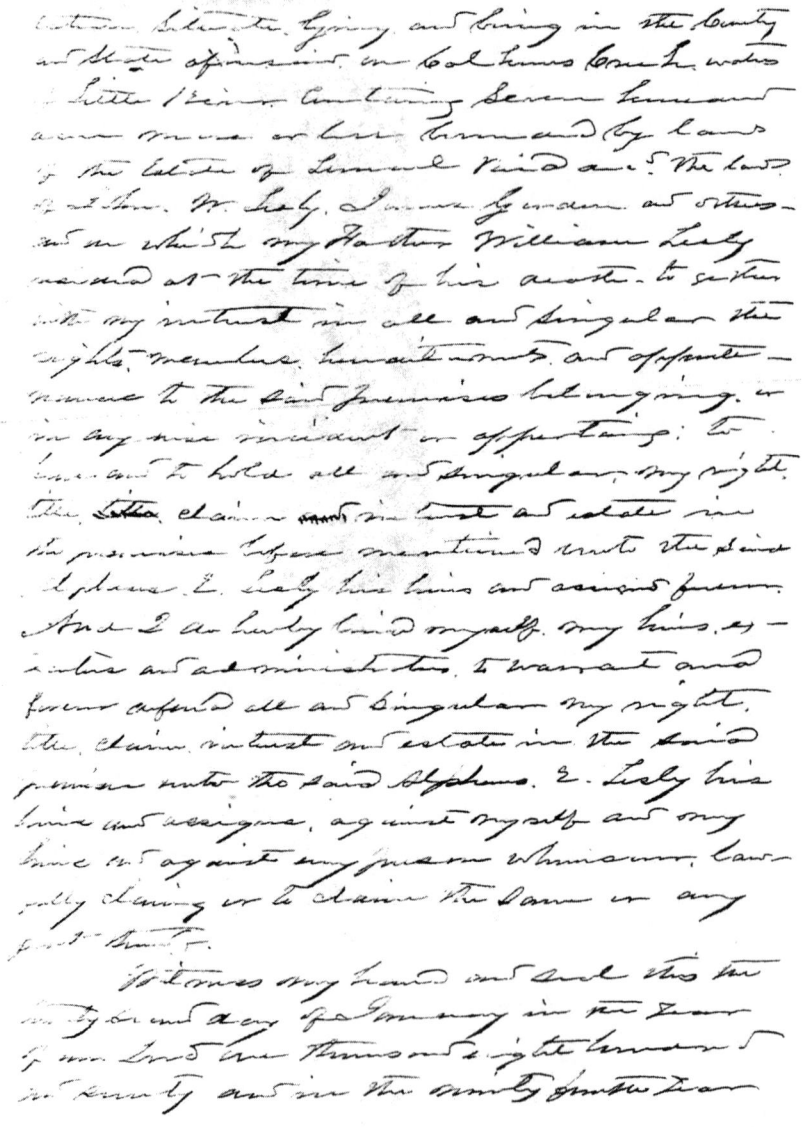

The State of South Carolina.
Abbeville County.

Whereas William Leslie late of
the County and State aforesaid by the
Eighth clause of his last will and
testament, which bears date the fourth
day of February in the year of our Lord
one thousand eight hundred and sixty
is on record in the office of Probate
of this County, gave the plantation
on which he then resided, and of which
he died seized and possessed to his
sons Alpheus E. Leslie and John I. Leslie
And whereas the said John I. Leslie has
let a his interest in said plantation
to his brother the said Alpheus Leslie,
in desirous of making a convey-
ance of said interest to his said brother

Now Know all men by these
presents that I the said John I. Leslie
in consideration of the sum of one thousand five hundred dollars to me paid
by Alpheus E. Leslie, have granted, bargained, sold and released and by these
presents do grant bargain, sell, release
and convey unto the said Alpheus E.
Leslie all my undivided right, title,
claim, interest and estate in that plan-

STATE OF SOUTH CAROLINA)
)
COUNTY OF ABBEVILLE.   )   LAST WILL AND TESTAMENT.

IN THE NAME OF GOD, AMEN.

I, W.E. Leslie of Abbeville County, South Carolina, do make, ordain, publish and declare this as and for my last will and testament.

Item I. I commit my soul to the gracious God who gave it, and direct that my body shall be interred according to the rites of the Presbyterian Church and that a suitable monument be erected to mark my grave, and that all expense incurred therefor be paid out of my estate.

Item II. I will and direct that my executors hereinafter named shall pay all of my just debts with the first money coming into hands.

Item III. I will, devise and bequeath to my beloved wife, Annie A. Leslie for and during her natural life all of my proper both real and personal, for her maintenance and support, this provision being in lieu of all claim of dower or other interests in or to all real estate which I shall die seized and possessed of. Upon the death of my wife I direct that all of my property then remaining be sold and the proceeds divided among my childr Annie Donald, Nicholas, James, Mac, Robert, Sarah, John, Virgini David, Alpheus and Albert, since I have already made advances t Frank and William Jr. in the approximate sums of Three Thousand ($3,000.00) Dollars each, for which I do not demand any account Since Sarah, Virginia, and Alpheus received a college education I direct that their shares be one-half as great as the shares c Annie Donald, Nicholas, James, Mac, Robert, John, David and Alt

Item IV. Whereas my son Mac is now looking after the farm and continue to do so and I feel that if, as a result of his effor he keeps the installments and taxes upon the place paid he shou receive credit out of the sale of the place to the extent of the principal of the mortgage indebtedness and taxes paid by him, I direct that this be done. Sould another son take his place I direct that he receive the same consideration.

Item V. I appoint my wife, Annie H. Leslie, executrix, and my son, W.E. Leslie, Jr., executor of this my last will and testamen with full power to do any and all things necessary for the carrying out of the terms of this instrument including the right to convey both real and personal property without the Order of the Court either at public or private sale and I direct that they not be required to give bond.

In witness whereof, I hereunto set my hand and seal this 14th day of March, 1939.

W. E. Leslie (Seal)

Signed, sealed, published and
declared by W.E. Leslie as and
for his last will and testament
in the presence of us, who in
his presence, and of each other,
at his request have subscribed
our names as witnesses.

M A Durkint Address *Abbeville, S.C.*

N J Evans Address *Abbeville, S.C.*

James R. Hill Address *Abbeville, S.C.*

INVENTORY AND APPRAISEMENT OF PERSONAL PROPERTY OF THE ESTATE

OF - - - Willie (W.E.) Leslie, Deceased.

Articles	Face Value		Appraised Value
Insurance payable to the Estate	$397.21	- - -	$ 397.21
Household furniture	$500.00	- - -	$ 500.00
Five mules	$500.00	- - -	$ 500.00
Two Mares	$200.00	- - -	$ 200.00
Two Colts	$100.00.	- - -	$ 100.00
Three Cows and One Bull	$125.00	- - -	$ 125.00
1 calf	$ 10.00	- - -	$ 10.00
Lower & Rake	$ 20.00	- - -	$ 20.00
Wagon	$ 10.00	- - -	$ 10.00
Lot of Farm tools	$ 70.00	- - -	$ 70.00
Lot of Sheep	$100.00	- - -	$ 100.00
Total	- - - - - - - - -		$2032.21

-REAL ESTATE-

Description	Assessed Value		Appraised Value
525 Acres in Reids School District, Abbeville County - - - - - - - -	$2960.00	......	$6,000.00

(Mortgaged to Federal Land Bank
for $4,000.00)

True Copy:
August 30th, 1940.

Judge of Probate.

THOMAS LESLY - No. W 381   WIDOW MARY - CONTAINS BIBLE RECORD

Monroe Co., Tenn. 25 Nov. 1832 - appeared before Chas F. Keith,
Circuit Judge Thomas Lesly, a resident of McMinn Co., - aged 72
yrs the 15th April last - the reasons that he does not make application in said McMinn Co are the following to wit he lives on the
county line with part of his land in McMinn and part in Monroe but
he lives nearer to seat of justice of Monroe than McMinn and one
of his witnesses to wit Magness Tullock is old and infirm and lives
in Blount Co. and was not willing to go as far as seat of justice of
McMinn Co. Thomas Lesly was born in County Antrim, Ireland on 15
April 1760, his father removed to S. C. when he, Thomas, was a
small boy, - he was living in 96 District in S. C. now Abbyville Co
when called into service - he volunteered there as a minute man for
12 months under Capt. Joseph Pickens in Col. Andrew Pickens Reg.-
rendezvoused at Thomas Lesly's in said 96 dist.- marched to 96 now
called Cambridge - returned to place of rendezvous and lay there for
some time then marched to the Rocky Spring in quest of Daniel Mc-
Girt (?) and his company of Tories- they fled - returned to place
of rendezvous for some time- marched to Eames's field against the
Cherokee Indians- lay there for some time about 2 or 3 months -
returned to former place of rendezvous lay there some time and
scouted the country after Tories and Indians until his time was up-
again while living at some place in Dec. 1780 he volunteered in
the cavalry under Col. Andrew Pickens (had no Capt) - met together
or rendezvoused on Clark (looks/more/like/Clark/than/Clark) and
McCall's tract in the Indian land- marched to Rutherford Co., N. C.
where he amongst others was ordered to guard a quantity of Negroes,
horses and other property belonging to the Americans into Mecklenber
Co. - returned and joined Col. Pickens at the Cowpens on the day
of the battle there- Gen. Morgan was commander in chief on that day,
put under the command of Capt Robert Anderson and they guarded a
forge wagon and some wounded men to Gibbertstown in Rutherford Co
N. C.- then guarded British prisoners to Catawba river- marched to
Meckeenberg (McLinburgh) co. and then to meet Col. Pickens who
he believes was made Genl. the next day after the said battle- this
was their order but they attempted to join Genl. Pickens at the
widow Torrances in Roan Co- it was on the day that the British
crossed the Catawba river when they came in sight of Genl. Pickens
men- Col. Tarleton's troops came between then and Genl. Pickens
company and Genl. Pickens had to retreat one way and they the
other. Gen. Pickens went on and fought the battle of Guilford and
they joined him immediately after that battle in Mecklenberg Co.
when on his way to S. C.-marched with him until they crossed
Broad River when Capt. Anderson was promoted to Col. - Gen. Pickins
then ordered Col. Anderson Col. Clark and Col. McCall to march by
way of Cherokee ford and Savannah river into Ga. and take no Tory
prisoners but if they found any that needed killing not to spare
them - Lesly went under command of Col. Anderson- the companies
separated to meet at the Cherokee ford - they killed 12 tories and
met at appointed place- there was a number of Tories killed at that
time- then marched thru Ga. and on to Abbyville S. C.- there Robt.
Carrethers was made Capt.- marched thru the country to surprise
the Tories and/thru/the into the Indian country to surprise them -
there was no safety at home and the only security was in being unde
arms - then under the command of Capt. Joseph Pickins marched to
the seige of Ninety-six where Gen. Green was commander in chief
and here Capt. Pickins got mortally wounded- then they went into

Abbyville to guard the settlement while they reaped their wheat-
joined Gen. Pickins agin there - put under command of Capt. Moses
Liddle, marched to Bacon's bridge and joined Genl. Green's army-
Genl. Pickins army lay about 1 mi. below the bridge and Genl. Green'
about 7 mi.- lay there until he was discharged in July 1782.

Lesly lived at the same place where he entered the service (Pendill
(Abbyville Co) about 3 years after the Rev.- removed into Pendillon
Pendleton Dist S. C. where he lived until 1819 and then to McMinn
Co.

Preston Starrett and John Robertson of Monroe Co are witnesses

Magniss Tulloch of Blount Co. aged 68 certifies that he became
acquainted with Thomas Lesly in 96 Dist now Abbeville Co S. C.
about 1777 and served with him in Rev. War -

McMinn Co., Tenn. 2 Mar 1844 Thomas Lesly aged 39 states that he
is the son of Thomas Lesly the pensioner and that his father died
22 Feb. 1839 leaving a widow and the following named children/
that are surviving : James, Samuel, Mary Ann, Thomas. He states
that his mother died 18 Aug 1843 - this declaration is made to
obtain the pension due the widow at her death - that the bible
record is in the handwriting of Thomas Lesly.
Moses A. Cass states that he saw the family record taken from the
Presbyterian Church Government marked letter B on the back of the
record(Note: Why letter B ?)

        BIBLE RECORD
   Jane (?) M. Lesly b. 13 Oct 1783
   Wm. Harris Lesly b 15 Jan 1786 (?)
   John Lesly b. 16 Dec 1787
  Peggy W. Lesly b. 10 Feb 1790
  James Lesly b. 23 Apr 1792
  Samuel Lesly b. 13 Oct 1795
  Maryann Lesly b 22 July 1798
  Andrew Lesly b 31 Oct 1800
  Rebeccah Lesly b 8 Oct 1802
  Thomas Lesly 27 Jan 1805   )   in different handwriting
  Juliana McNabb b 4 Nov 1810   )

NAMES: Chasl F. Keith ; Magness Tulloch; Capt. Joseph Pickens;
Col. Andrew Fickens; Daniel McGirt(?); Gen. Morgan; Capt. Robert
Anderson; Gen. Andrew Pickins; Col. Tarleton; Col. Robert Anderson;
Col. Clark; Col. McCall; Capt. Robert Carruthers; Gen. Green;
Capt. Moses Liddle; Major John Bowie; Capt. John Moore; Major Thos.
Faro; Lt. Samuel Arels (?) ; Capt. Benj. Tutt (?); Preston Starritt;
John Robertson; Joseph Hockney; John Hughs; James Hamilton; Alex.
Gay; John B. Tipton; E. H. Wear; Capt. John Cowan; James
Standefer, member of Congress; Wm. C. Easton; Thomas Lesly, Jr.;
Mary Lesly widow; James Lesly; Samuel Lesly; Mary Ann Lesly;
Moses A. Cass; J. C. Carlock

127

GENERAL AFFIDAVIT.

State of _Florida_, County of _Madison_, ss:

In the matter of _claim of James T. Leslie for survivor service pension, Indian War, # 1343_

ON THIS _13_ day of _January_ A. D. 189_2_ personally appeared before me a _Notary Public_ in and for the aforesaid County duly authorized to administer oaths, _James T. Leslie_ aged _77_ years, a resident of _____ in the County of _Madison_ and State of _Florida_ well known to me to be reputable and entitled to credit, and who, being duly sworn, declared in relation to aforesaid case as follows:

[Note.—Affiants should state how they gain a knowledge of the facts to which they testify.]

I am the applicant & claimant in this claim; my grandfather was an old Irishman & he always signed his name "Lesly"; my father spelled his name the same way, and I wrote it that way myself until about 25 years ago; I changed it because my uncle in Abbeville & an older brother of mine spelled the name "Leslie", and I thought I would change mine likewise as I thought it looked the prettiest; my relations in Alabama sign their name "Lesly", & when I write them I sign "Lesly"; my full name is James Thomas Lesly or "Leslie" as I afterwards wrote it; I think the name of the person who obtained my land warrant for me was Robertson Sessions, & I afterwards sold the warrant to him too of my comrade Jordan Rutherford & Nathan King.

H __ Post Office address is _Madison, Fla_

_____ further declare that _____ no interest in said case and _____ not concerned in its prosecution.

Attest: L. Vann.

T. T. Leslie

[If Affiants sign by mark, two persons who can write sign here.] — *[Signature of Affiants.]*

Witness our hand the year and day above written.

[Signature of Agent.]

DISTRICT OF COLUMBIA, CITY OF WASHINGTON, ss:

Personally came J. H. SOULÉ, representing the firm of SOULE & CO., whom I know to be the person he represents himself to be, and who, having signed above acceptance of agreement, acknowledged the same to be their free act and deed.

Witness my hand and seal this _13"_ day of _Nov^r_ 189_2_

[L.S.] (NOTARY PUBLIC.)

Commissioner's Approval.

APPROVED FOR , _____ DOLLARS and payable to SOULE & CO., of Washington, D. C., the recognized attorneys.

Commissioner of Pensions.

INDIAN WARS.

Claim of Soldier for Service Pension Under Act of July 27, 1892.

To be executed before some officer authorized to administer oaths for general purposes. The official character and signature of any such officer not required by law to use a seal must be certified by the clerk of the proper court, giving dates of beginning and close of official term.

A full and explicit reply is required to all questions indicated by this blank.

State of *Florida*, County of *Madison*, ss:

ON THIS *24* day of *August*, A. D. one thousand eight hundred and ninety *Two*, personally appeared before me, a *Notary Public* in and for the County and State aforesaid, *James T. Lesly*, aged *79* years, a resident of *Madison Co.* in the State of *Florida*, who, being duly sworn according to law, declares that he is the identical person who served under the name of *James T. Lesly*, as a *private* in the company commanded by Captain *Thos. Langford*, the ____ Regiment of ____ Regiment, commanded by *Col. Wm. J. Baily*, in the *Fla. Seminole Indian* War; that he enlisted at *Madison C.H. Flo*, on or about the ____ day of *September*, A. D. 18 *39*, for the term of *Six months*, and was honorably discharged at *Willcut's Langford 10 miles S. of Madison*, on the ____ day of *January*, A. D. 18 *40*; that he also served in *Langford's* Co. *Baily's* Regt., ____ Vols., from *Jan* 18 *40*, to *May* 18 *40*; and in ____ Co., ____ Regt., ____ Vols., from ____, 18 ___, to ____, 18 ___; that he has not been employed in the military or naval service of the United States otherwise than as stated above.

That at the time of entering the service claimed for he was *26* years of age, *6* feet *2* inches in height, with *gray* eyes, *sandy* hair, *fair* complexion, by occupation a *farmer* and that he was born at *Abbeville* County of *Abbeville* State of *South Carolina*. That since leaving the service he has resided at *Pontotoc, Miss., 3 years & 2 mo.*, at ____ years, at ____ years, at ____ years, and at *Madison ever since Apr. 1839*. That he was married to *Mary Server*, on the ____ day of *July*, A. D. 18 *42*, at *Madison Co. Fla.* that his said wife is now *dead*, having died on the *4* day of *May*, A. D. 18 *83*; that he has *never* since remarried, and that the maiden name of his present wife was ____

That he has *never* heretofore made application for pension, the number of his claim being ____; that he has ____ heretofore made application for bounty land, the number of his land warrant being *& obtained it for 16 ac.*

That he is a citizen of the United States, and makes this application for the purpose of obtaining a pension under the provisions of the Act approved July 27, 1892, and he hereby appoints *Soulè & Co.* of *Washington, D.C.*, his true and lawful attorneys.

That his post-office address is No. ____ street, (city or town of) *Madison C.H.*, County of *Madison*, State of *Florida*

James T Leslie
(Signature of Claimant in full.)

ATTEST: *J. T. Ellison*
E. J. Vann
Livingston Vann, Notary Public in for the State of Fla.

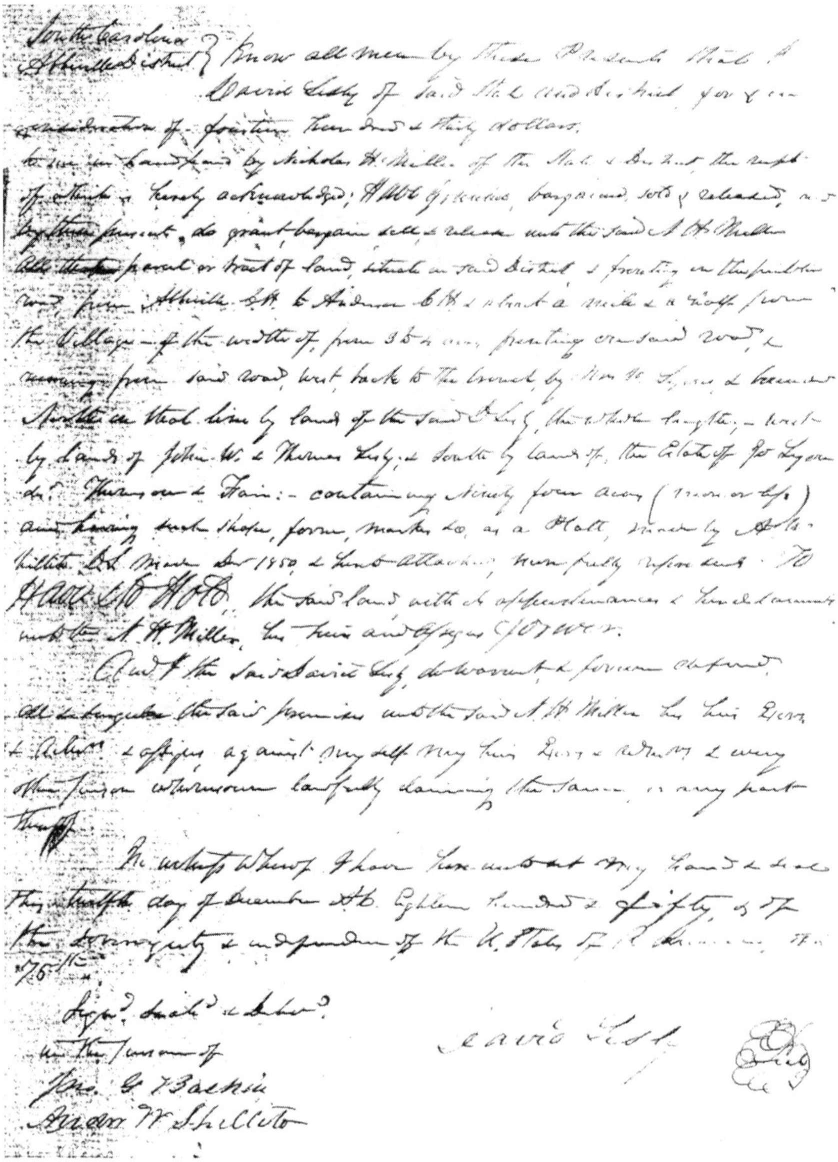

South Carolina } Know all men by these Presents that I
Abbeville District } David Lesly of said State and District for & in
consideration of fourteen hundred & thirty dollars,
to me in hand paid by Nicholas H. Miller of the State & District the receipt
of which is hereby acknowledged; Have granted, bargained, sold & released, and
by these presents do grant, bargain, sell & release unto the said N. H. Miller
All that parcel or tract of land, situate in said District & fronting on the public
road from Abbeville C.H. to Anderson C.H. & about a mile & a half from
the Village — of the width of, from 35 to [illegible] fronting on said road, &
running from said road west, back to the branch, by [illegible] & bounded
North on that line by land of the said D. Lesly, the whole length, — west
by land of John W. & Thomas Lesly, & South by land of the Estate of [illegible] Lyon
dec.d Thomson & Fair: — containing Ninety four acres (more or less)
and having such shape, form, marks &c, as a Platt, made by A. H.
Miller D.S. made Dec 1850 & hereto attached, more fully represents. To
Have and to Hold, the said land with its appurtenances & hereditaments
unto the N. H. Miller, his heirs and Assigns forever.

And I the said David Lesly do warrant & forever defend
all & singular the said premises unto the said N. H. Miller his heirs Exors
& Admrs & assigns against myself my heirs Exors & Admrs & every
other person whomsoever lawfully claiming the same or any part
thereof.

In witness whereof I have hereunto set my hand & seal
this twelfth day of December A.D. Eighteen hundred & fifty, & of
the sovereignty & independence of the U. States of America the
75th.

Signed sealed & delivered
in the presence of
Jno. G. Baskin
Andrew W. Shillito

David Lesly (seal)

GENERATION EIGHT

(Five great-grandchildren of Thomas and Jane Lesslie)
(Four great-grandchildren of William and Ann Caldwell Lesly)
(Three great-grandchildren of William and Martha Emily White Lesly)
(Two great-grandchildren of Alpheus Ezekiel and Virginia Miller Lesly)
(Great-grandchildren of William Edwin and Annie Henry Leslie)
(Grandchildren of William Edwin Jr. and Glendel Bowen Leslie)

The children of Marcellene and William Chambers (Red) Myers

1.1.8.4.1.1.2.1 – William (Dub) Chambers Myers, Jr. – b. July 19, 1951.

1.1.8.4.1.1.2.2 – Marcellene (Sissy) Leslie Myers – b. Nov. 21, 1953.

1.1.8.4.1.1.2.3 – Leisa Weston – b. July 7, 1957.

1.1.8.4.1.1.2.4 – Melissa Westbury – b. Sept. 11, 1960.

1.1.8.4.1.1.2.5 – Laurie Leslie – b. Apr. 29, 1964.

Grandchildren of Alpheus Ezekiel and Lucy Sturdivant Leslie

The child of Robert Edward and Jane Moore Leslie

1.1.8.4.1.3.1.1 – Martha Ann – b. Sept. 30. She gradu-ated from Mountain Brook High School, Birmingham, Alabama and University of Mississippi (Ole Miss), then worked for "Relax the Back" for several years. Married Michael Alley and they have two children; now living in Greenville, South Carolina. The children of Donald William and Marian Henderson Leslie.

The children of Donald William and Marian Henderson Leslie

1.1.8.4.1.3.3.1 – Susan Kaye – b. Dec. 25, 1957. Susan graduated from Dunwoody High School, Dekalb County, Georgia and graduated from the Licensed Practical Nurse Program, Dekalb High School; H H Tech. She practiced at Grady Memorial Hospital in Atlanta, where she met her future husband, Dr. Michael R. Vaughn. They have two daughters. She is now a licensed dog trainer, living in Atlanta, Georgia.

1.1.8.4.1.3.3.2 – Donald William, Jr. (Bo) – b. Sept. 7, 1959, d. March 27, 1973. Bo was the typical red headed boy that found his share of trouble to get into but always charmed his way out of each situation. He was a happy boy that touched many lives, but his life was cut short by an automobile accident.

1.1.8.4.1.3.3.3 – Henry Miller (Hank) – b. Jan. 10, 1961, d. Oct. 19, 2011. Hank graduated from Dunwoody High School, Dekalb County, Georgia and from the University of Georgia. He was employed by Edwards Life Services selling medical equipment to hospitals for operating room use. He married Mary Allen and they lived on a small farm with horses, goats and other critters until complications from a knee replacement operation took his life. They had no children.

The children of James and Mary Sturdivant Leslie Williams

1.1.8.4.1.3.3.4.1 – Mary Jeanne Williams – b. June 26, 1956. Born in Charleston, South Carolina, she was adopted by Mary and Jim Williams, and graduated from Jackson High School, Jackson, South Carolina. She moved to Portland,

Oregon and married Bruce Empey. They have two children. She is a Nurse Practitioner. They are now living in Oregon, but are planning to move to Greenville, South Carolina.

1.1.8.4.1.3.3.4.2 – Leslie Lynne Williams – b. Dec. 12, 1962. She graduated from Jackson High School, Jackson, South Carolina and then from Clemson University and MUSC and worked as an Occupational Therapist. She is married to Osman A. Hicklin III (Bud) and they have two sons.

1.1.8.4.1.3.3.4.3 – Laura Elizabeth Williams – b. Dec. 4, 1965. She graduated from Wren High School in Piedmont, South Carolina and Greensboro College in Greensboro, North Carolina. She worked as a Dental Hygienist and has entered Clemson University in the Masters program of Science. She is unmarried.

1.1.8.4.1.3.3.4.4 – Lucy Jana Williams – b. Sept. 30, 1971. She graduated from Middleton High, Charleston, South Carolina and from Western Governor's University. She married Tim Ramsey, divorced and married Ed Nelson and they have two children. Joined U.S Air Force then became substitute teacher. She lives in Colorado with plans to move to South Carolina upon husband's retirement.

Grandchildren of Albert Henry and Sydelle Graves Leslie

The children of Harold and Jean Ellen Leslie Winters

1.1.8.4.1.4.1.1 – Harold Hutson Winters, Jr. (Hal) – b. Feb. 14, 1952.

1.1.8.4.1.4.1.2 – Leslie Ann Winters – b. May 24, 1955.

The children of Frank A and Margaret Sydelle Leslie Meyer

1.1.8.4.4.2.1 – Martin Leslie Meyer – b. Dec. 23, 1956.

1.1.8.4.4.2.2 – Jeffery Frederick Meyer – b. May 2, 1958, d. 1979.

1.1.8.4.4.2.3 – Wendy Elizabeth Meyer – b. Feb. 14, 1962.

The children of George Johnson and Ann Henry Leslie Maust

1.1.8.4.4.2.1 – Kimbal Ann – b. Sept. 18, 1957.

1.1.8.4.4.2.2 – Gregory Allen – b. April 30 1959, d. Nov. 6, 2005.

1.1.8.4.4.2.3 – Robert Johnson (Jay) – b. July 16, 1973.

Grandchildren of John Donnald and Georgia Philbert Leslie

The children of Donnald Philbert and Elizabeth Leslie

1.1.8.4.1.7.1.1

The children of George Amos and Margaret Ann (Peggy) Leslie Pierce

1.1.8.4.1.7.2.1 – Leslie Ann Pierce – b. Dec. 24, 1965. She works as an Administrator for the Columbia Museum of Art.

1.1.8.4.1.7.2.2 – Patricia (Patty) Ann Pierce – b. Jan. 12, 1967. She owns her own business as a lobbyist for conservation issues.

1.1.8.4.1.7.2.3 – Virginia (Ginny) Ann Pierce – b. June 30, 1971. She is an archeologist and has completed graduate school at the University of South Carolina.

Grandchildren of Rudolph S.A. and Sarah Ellen Leslie Thunberg

The children of Rudolph and Deborah Ann Jamroz Thunberg

1.1.8.4.1.8.2.1 – Ellen Leslie Thunberg – b. Aug. 11, 1986.

Grandchildren of Robert Hall and Dorothy Nickles Leslie

The children of Robert Hall, Jr. (Bobbie) and Caroline Bell Leslie

1.1.8.4.1.9.1.1 – Robert Ted – b. April 6, 1963.

1.1.8.4.1.9.1.2 – Debra Carol (Debbie) – b. March 24, 1966.

1.1.8.4.1.9.1.3 – Denis Scott – b. Aug. 1, 1968.

The children of Charles Edwin and Christine Goodenough Leslie

1.1.8.4.1.9.2.1 – Tina Marie – b. Aug. 29, 1962.

1.1.8.4.1.9.2.2 – Michael Charles – b. Nov. 27, 1965.

The children of Benny Richard and Mary Louise Davis

1.1.8.4.1.9.4.1 – Leslie Lynn – b. Nov. 15, 1969.

1.1.8.4.1.9.4.2 – Karen Suzanne – b. May 10, 1977.

Grandchildren of James and Martha Wilson Leslie

The children of James and Gertrude Fox Leslie

1.1.8.4.1.11.1.1 – Jennifer Denise Leslie – b. May 13, 1970. Graduated from Irmo, South Carolina High School, University of South Carolina with B.A. Psychology, LPN degree, and Real Estate degree. She is now living in Columbia, South Carolina following a real estate career.

The children of Franklin Eugene and Marie Ann Pursley

1.1.8.4.1.11.2.1 – Carole Lynn – b. Feb, 22, 1970. She graduated from Brentwood High School, Nashville, Tennessee, Jacksonville University with B.A. in Education, University of Central Florida with a degree from School of Psychology. She married Gary Goss and has two children.

1.1.8.4.1.11.2.2 – Leigh Ann – b. March 20, 1973. She graduated from Brentwood High School, Nashville, Tennessee and Florida State University with B.A. in Psychology, AIU, Atlanta, GA with a Masters Degree in Information Technology. She married Igor Zikus.

The children of Henry Stephen and Connie Price Leslie

1.1.8.4.1.11.3.1 – Scott Stephen – b. April 3, 1974. He graduated from Seneca High School and College of

Charleston and is employed by UPS. He lives in Peachtree City, Georgia and is interested in golf and dogs. He is married to Kimberly Schultz and has no children.

1.1.8.4.1.11.3.2 – Alison Michelle – b. Feb. 23, 1977. She graduated from Seneca High School and Appalachian State University. Started a career in Health, Food & Nutrition, and now is employed by University of South Carolina Pediatric Specialty Clinic. Married to Shawn Hanna and they have one child and currently live in Lancaster, South Carolina.

1.1.8.4.1.11.3.3 – Amanda Brook – b. Aug. 31, 1980. Graduated from Seneca High School and Winthrop University; now employed by Clemson University, College of Engineering and Science-Student online communications. Married to Daniel Harris and currently lives on Lake Keowee and has no children.

1.1.8.4.1.11.3.4 – Todd Michael – b. June 1, 1984. Graduated from Seneca High School and from Greenville Tech Automotive. Interested in sports and scouting (Eagle Scout), now in custom cars. He is currently living in Nashville, Tennessee.

Grandchildren of Nicholas Miller and Mary Edwards Leslie

The children of Nicholas Miller, Jr. (Nicky) and Pamela Sue North Leslie

1.1.8.4.1.12.1.1 – Mary Elizabeth Leslie – b. May 30, 1983. Graduated from Leon High School, Tallahassee, Florida and University of North Florida, in Jacksonville. She worked as a reporter, but now is the Deputy Director of Communications, Florida Dept. of Management Services. She lives in Tallahassee, Florida.

1.1.8.4.1.12.1.2 – Andrew North Leslie – b. Nov. 25, 1986. Graduated from Leon High School, Tallahassee, Florida. He is a Blue Grass musician (as his father was) as a guitarist and repairs stringed instruments and lives in Tallahassee.

The child of W. Thomas and Robin Ann Leslie Copeland

1.1.8.4.1.12.2.1 – Casey Elizabeth Copeland – b. 1983.

Grandchildren of Uriah Franklin and Annie Donnald Leslie Corkrum

The children of Roger and Virginia Ann Corkrum Hope

1.1.8.4.1.13.1.1 – Steven Uriah Hope – b. Nov. 18, 1975.

1.1.8.4.1.13.1.2 – Nathaniel Wallace – b. July 4, 1977.

1.1.8.4.1.13.1.3 – Natalie Ann – b. May 16, 1979.

1.1.8.4.1.13.1.4 – Maribeth Ann – b. Dec. 25, 1980.

1.1.8.4.1.13.1.5 – Alexander William – b. Nov. 8, 1982.

1.1.8.4.1.13.1.6 – Sarah Marie – b. April 18, 1985.

1.1.8.4.1.13.1.7 – John David – b. Aug. 2, 1987.

1.1.8.4.1.13.1.8 – Samuel _____ – b. _____

The children of Uriah Franklin (Frank) Jr. and Kay Johnson Corkrum

1.1.8.4.1.13.2.1 – Kevin Hudson – b. June 2, 1985.

1.1.8.4.1.13.2.2 – Patrick Lee – b. March 29, 1988.

GENERATION NINE

(Six great-grandchildren of Thomas and Jane Lesslie)
(Five great-grandchildren of William and Ann Caldwell Lesly)
(Four great-grandchildren of William and Martha Emilly White Lesly)
(Three great-grandchildren of Alpheus Ezekiel and Virginia Miller Lesly)
(Two great-grandchildren of William Edwin and Annie Henry Lesly)
(Great-grandchildren of William Edwin, Jr. and Glendel Bowen Leslie)
(Grandchildren of William (Red) Chambers and Marcelene Leslie Myers)

The child of William Chambers, Jr. and Laura Belmont Myers

1.1.8.4.1.1.2.1.1 – William (Will) Belmont – b. Sept. 6, 1986.

1.1.8.4.1.1.2.1.2 – Kathryn – b. Feb. 21, 1991. Graduated from Oakwood Academy 7 attending Winthrop University. She plays soccer, works with autistic children and human nutrition.

1.1.8.4.1.1.2.1.3 – Nickolas (Nick) – b. Feb. 1994. Graduated from Spartanburg High School & plans to attend Spartanburg Methodist.

The children of James &Leisa Myers Knotts

1.1.8.4.1.1.2.2.1 – Weston Leslie Myers – b. Nov. 3, ____. Graduated Greenwood High School, attended Lander University and is interested in computer technology. Now working for Research In Motion (Rin) and living in Irving, Texas.

The children of Bryan & Laurie Myers Cordell

1.1.8.4.1.1.2.3.1 – Addie Glendel – b. Sept. 20, 1996. She is attending Greenwood Christian School; plays soccer and likes to study history.

1.1.8.4.1.1.2.3.2 – Alexandria (Lexi) Ruth – b. May 24, 2005. Attending Ninety-Six Middle School

Great-grandchildren of Alpheus Ezekiel and Lucy Sturdivant Leslie
Grandchildren of Robert Edward and Jane Moore Leslie

The children of Michael Wayne and Martha Ann Leslie All

1.1.8.4.1.3.1.1.1 – Edward Warren Alley – b. ____; Graduated from _____ High School and College of Charleston. Works for Pilot Travel Centers and lives in Knoxville, Tennessee.

1.1.8.4.1.3.1.1.2 – Jane Leslie Alley – b. 1982. Graduated from High School and Clemson University; Works for NETC as a travel group coordinator. Now living in Boston, Massachusetts.

Grandchildren of Donald William and Marian Henderson Leslie

The children of Michael Roy and Susan Kay Leslie Vaughn

1.1.8.4.3.3.1.1 – Allison Leslie Vaughn – b. Jan.1, 1987. Graduated from Grady high school, Atlanta, Georgia and George Washington University. Now enrolled at Georgia State University law school. She participated in competitive ice skating and swimming.

1.1.8.4.3.3.1.2 – Audrey Katherine Vaughn – b. Nov. 20, 1993. Graduated from Grady high school and planning

to enroll at University of Georgia fall of 2012. Member of her high school soccer team throughout her high school years. She is very interested in photography.

Grandchildren of James Haddon and Mary Sturdivant Leslie Williams

The children of Bruce and Mary Jeanne Williams Empey

1.1.8.4.3.4.1.1 – Breanne Empey – b.

1.1.8.4.3.4.1.2 – Taylor Empey – b.

The children of Osman A. (Bud) and Leslie Lynne Williams Hicklin III

1.1.8.4.3.4.2.1 – James Alexander (Alex) Hicklin – b.

1.1.8.4.3.4.2.2 – Evan Hicklin – b.

The child of Tim and Lucy Jana Williams Ramsey

1.1.8.4.3.4.4.1 – Jayce Ramsey – b. Sept 6, 1994.

The children of Ed and Lucy Jana Williams Nelson

1.1.8.4.1.3.4.4.2 – Riley Nelson – b. July 7, 1996.

1.1.8.4.1.3.4.4.3 – Kaytlin Nelson – b. May 5, 2003.

Great-Grandchildren of Albert Henry and Sedelle Graves Leslie
Grandchildren of Harold Hutson and Jeanne Ellen Leslie Winters

The child of Harold Hutson, Jr. and Susan Ford Randolph Winters

1.1.8.4.1.4.1.1.1 – Alan Michael Winters – b. 1985.

The children of Robert Gerald and Leslie Ann Winters Everitt

1.1.8.4.1.4.1.2.1 – Brian Ross Everitt – b. 1985.

1.1.8.4.1.4.1.2.2 – Kelly Jean Everitt – b. 1990.

Grandchildren of Frank Albert (Dutch) and Margaret Sydelle Meyer

The children of Martin Leslie Meyer and

1.1.8.4.1.4.2.1.1

1.1.8.4.1.4.2.1.2

The children of Windy Elizabeth Meyer and Joel Goodwin

1.1.8.4.1.4.2.2.1 – Andrew Heath – b. June 8, 1992. He graduated from Northern Vance H.S., Henderson, North Carolina and is now a junior at North Carolina State. Played soccer and tennis in H.S. Rebuilds autos - recent project changing a Honda automatic to stick shift.

1.1.8.4.1.4.2.2.2 – Isabelle Ellen – b. March 1, 1995. Presently attending Ker-Vance Academy, Henderson, North Carolina Level 7 gymnast, runs cross country, plays soccer and is a cheerleader. She likes to sew and has entered creations in state fairs for prizes.

Grandchildren of George Johnson and Ann Henry Leslie Maust, Jr.

The children of William and Kimbal Ann Maust Empson

1.1.8.4.1.4.3.1.1 – Justin R. – b. 1981.

1.1.8.4.1.4.3.1.2 – Jesse William – b. 1984.

1.1.8.4.1.4.3.1.3 – David

The children of Robert Johnson and Joanna Cecelia Thoren Maust

1.1.8.4.1.4.3.3.1 – Jacob Johnson Maust – b. 1998.

1.1.8.4.1.4.3.3.2 – Noah George Maust – b. 2000.

1.1.8.4.1.4.3.3.3 – Adam Olaf Maust – b. 2000.

1.1.8.4.1.4.3.3.4 – Emma Cecelia Maust – b. 2005.

Great-grandchildren of Robert Hall and Dorothy Nickles Leslie
Grandchildren of Robert Hall, Jr. and Martha Carolayn Bell Leslie

The children of Robert Ted and Lydia Mae Horton Leslie

1.1.8.1.4.9.1.1.1 – Lauren Nicole Leslie – b. 1996.

1.1.8.1.4.9.1.1.2 – Robert Nickles Leslie – b. 1998.

1.1.8.1.4.9.1.1.3 – Mitchel Benton Leslie – b. 2000.

The children of Rodney Brooks and Debra Carol Leslie Grizzle

1.1.8.1.4.9.1.2.1 – Parker Brooks Grizzle – b. 1996.

1.1.8.1.4.9.1.2.2 – Logan Carter Grizzle – b. 1998.

The children of Denis Scott and Nova Marie Leslie

1.1.8.4.1.9.1.3.1 – Samuel Scott Leslie – b. 2001.

1.1.8.4.1.9.1.3.2 – Mary Elizabeth Leslie – b. 2004.

Grandchildren of Charles Edward and Christine Scott Goodenough Leslie

The children of ———————- and Tina Marie Leslie Batchelor

1.1.8.4.1.9.2.1.1 – Christina Marie Batchelor – b. 1996.

The children of Michael Charles and Laura Kelling Leslie

1.1.8.4.1.9.2.2.1 – Carolyn Baker Leslie – b. 1998.

1.1.8.4.1.9.2.2.2 – Catherine Hope Leslie – b. 2000.

Grandchildren of Benny Richard and Mary Louise Davis

The children of George L. (Jay) III and Leslie Lynn Davis Johnson

1.1.8.4.1.9.4.1.1. – George Franklin Johnson (Buddy) – b. 1998.

1.1.8.4.1.9.4.1.2 – Landyn Nicole – b. 2002.

1.1.8.4.1.9.4.1.3 – Abby Grace – b. 2003.

1.1.8.4.1.9.4.1.4 – Hampton (Hamp)

The children of Chad Joseph and Karen Suzanne Heery

1.1.8.4.1.9.4.2.1 – Madison Louise – b. Jan. 30, 2006.

Great-Grandchildren of James Lewis and Martha Olivia Wilson Leslie
Grandchildren of Franklin Eugene and Marie Ann Leslie Pursley

The children of Gary and Carol Lynn Pursley Goss

1.1.8.4.1.11.2.1.1 – Grayson Holloway – b. 2000.

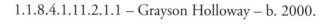

1.1.8.4.1.11.2.1.2 – Caroline Olivia – b. 2001.

Grandchildren of Henry Stephen & Connie Price Leslie

The children of Alison Michelle Leslie & Shawn Hanna

1.1.8.4.1.11.2.3.2.1 – Catherine Riggins – b. April 9, 2012.

Great-grandchildren of Uriah Franklin & Annie Donnald Leslie Corkrum
Grandchildren of Uriah Franklin, Jr. & Kay Johnson Corkrum

The children of Kevin Hudson & Diana Polanshek Corkrum

1.1.8.4.1.13.2.1.1 – Calvin Lee – b. March 3, 2011.

Descendants of Thomas Lesslie

```
1   Thomas Lesslie 1725 - 1778
.... +Jane 1725 - Unknown
....... 2   William Lesly 1754 - 1821
.............. +Ann Caldwell 1759 - 1800
.................. 3   Thomas Lesly 1780 - 1784
.................. 3   James Lesly 1782 - 1808
...................... +Eliza Bird Unknown - Unknown
.......................... 4   Caroline Lesly 1808 - 1868
................................ +James Van Ness 1808 - 1872
...................................... 5   Elizabeth Van Ness 1831 -
...................................... 5   Thomas Casey Van Ness 1847 -
.................. 3   John Harris Lesly 1784 - 1855
...................... +Mary Gilliland 1782 - 1856
.......................... 4   William Alexander Lesly 1806 -
.......................... 4   Leroy Gilliland Lesley 1807 - 1882
.............................. +Indianna Chiles Livingston 1809 - 1860
.................................... 5   John Thomas Lesly 1835 - 1913
........................................ +Margaret Adelaide Tucker 1838 -
............................................ 6   Indiana Elizabeth Lesly 1861 - 1939
............................................ 6   Emory Leroy Lesley 1864 - 1931
............................................ +Jennie K. Morgan
.................................................. 7   India Morgan Lesley 1897 - 1897
.................................................. 7   Margaret Lesley 1899 - 1899
.................................................. 7   Emory Leroy Lesley 1900 -
.................................................. +Carrie May Brawley
.................................................. 7   Mary Virginia Lesley 1906 -
.................................................. 7   Geraldine Elizabeth Lesley 1908 -
.................................................. +Arthur Allen Simpson
........................................................ 8   Nathan F. Simpson
........................................................ 8   Virginia Lesley Simpson
........................................................ 8   Allen Elizabeth Simpson
.................................................. 7   John Taliaferro Lesley 1910 - 2002
.................................................. +Louise Norton 1910 - 2006
........................................................ 8   India Louise Lesley 1941 -
........................................................ +Charles Silas Whedbee
........................................................ 8   John Taliaferro Lesley 1944 -
........................................................ 8   Susan Lesley 1947 -
........................................................ +James Wood Chandlee 1946 -
.............................................................. 9
.................................................. 7   India Chiles Lesley 1913 -
.................................................. +George Hogg Walker
........................................................ 8   George Lesley Walker 1936 -
.................................................. 7   Edyth Lesley 1916 -
.................................................. +Phillip Roy Secord
........................................................ 8   Edyth Blair Secord 1937 -
............................................ 6   John James Lesly 1868 - 1941
............................................ 6   William Taliaferro Lesley 1870 - 1904
............................................ +Sara R. Yancey 1870 -
.................................................. 7   Margaret Lesley 1899 -
.................................................. +James E. Montgomery
.................................................. 7   Sara Lesley 1903 -
.................................................. +Thomas Strong Moss
........................................................ 8   Sara Jane Moss 1926 -
............................................ 6   Theodore Lesley 1873 - 1942
............................................ +Carrie May Yancey
.................................................. 7   Theodore Livingston Lesley 1911 - 1978
.................................................. 7   Mary Lownes Lesley 1913 -
............................................ 6   Livingston Grillon Lesley 1877 -
............................................ +Georgia Florence Yancey
.................................................. 7   John Livingston Lesley 1899 -
.................................................. 7   Leona Lesley 1901 -
.................................................. +Dr. R.C. Wilson
........................................................ 8   Jean Wilson 1923 -
........................................................ 8   Lois Wilson 1925 -
.................................................. 7   Lois Earle Lesley 1905 -
.................................................. +Judson Butts Smith
........................................................ 8   Shirley Smith
.................................... 5   Emory Livingston Lesly 1837 - 1857
.................................... 5   Mary Camillus Lesly 1845 - 1927
.................................... +Rev. Urban Sinclair Bird
.................................... *2nd Husband of Mary Camillus Lesly:
.................................... +William Henry Brown 1842 - 1870
............................................ 6   William Lesley Brown 1869 -
.................................... *2nd Wife of Leroy Gilliland Lesley:
```

```
..................................... +Lucy Jane Sandwich 1825 - 1879
.......................................... 5   Emma Celestia Lesley 1862 - 1889
................................................ +William James Frierson 1858 - 1918
...................................................... 6   Lesley Law Frierson 1905 -
.......................................................... +Guy Leroy Buell
.................................................................. 7   William Harry Buell
...................................................................... 7   Guy Leroy Buell
............................................................................ 7   Margaret Louise Buell
........................ 4   Moses Taggart Lesly 1809 -
........................ 4   Theodore Josephus Lesly 1811 - 1890
.................................. +Rebecca Joel Brock 1818 - 1907
........................................ 5   Mary F. Lesly 1840 - 1840
........................................ 5   Margaret Ann Lesly 1841 -
.............................................. +Elic Burns  - 1874
.................................................... 6   David Josephus Burns 1864 -
.......................................... *2nd Husband of Margaret Ann Lesly:
................................................ +James B. Clark
...................................................... 6   Matthew Tuttle Clark 1876 -
............................................................ +Lillian A. Pennington
.................................................................. 7   Maggie Lucille Clark 1909 -
........................................................................ +L. J. Rye
.............................................................................. 8   Robbie Gray Rye 1927 -
.................................................................................. 8   Clark Rye 1935 -
.................................................................. 7   Annie Ruth Clark 1912 -
........................................................................ +Dudley Otts
.............................................................................. 8   J.D. Otts 1930 -
.............................................................................. 8   Jack Otts 1931 -
.............................................................................. 8   Kenneth Otts 1933 -
.............................................................................. 8   Mildred Otts 1936 -
.............................................................................. 8   Larry Otts 1938 -
.................................................................. 7   Clyde Clark 1917 -
........................................................................ +Era Fay Burks
.............................................................................. 8   James Hunter Clark 1937 -
.............................................................................. 8   Clyde Russel Clark 1938 -
...................................................... 6   Mary Lou Clark
............................................................ +William M. Comer
.................................................................. 7   Flora Comer
.................................................................. 7   Vera Comer
.................................................................. 7   Hazel Comer
.................................................................. 7   Oma Comer
.................................................................. 7   Lonnie Comer
.................................................................. 7   Corinne Comer
.................................................................. 7   David Comer
.................................................................. 7   Marie Comer
.................................................................. 7   Dudley Comer
........................................ 5   Samuel B. Lesly 1842 -
........................................ 5   Martin Brock Lesly 1844 -
........................................ 5   Susan Elizabeth Lesly 1845 -
.............................................. +X. H. Bagley
.................................................... 6   Eola Bagley
.................................................... 6   Susan Bagley
........................................ 5   Hannah Caroline Lesly 1847 -
.............................................. +Peter Newton Hughes 1847 - 1913
.................................................... 6   Luther Lesly Hughes 1870 -
.................................................... 6   Annie Laura Hughes 1872 -
.................................................... 6   Eula Lee Hughes 1874 -
.................................................... 6   John Leonard Hughes 1876 -
.................................................... 6   William Perry Hughes 1877 -
.................................................... 6   James Howard Hughes 1879 -
.................................................... 6   Mattie Lou Hughes 1881 -
.................................................... 6   Charles Arthur Hughes 1883 -
.................................................... 6   Cora Esta Hughes 1885 -
.................................................... 6   Emmit Hughes 1888 -
........................................ 5   Mary E. Lesly 1848 -
........................................ 5   John Harris Lesley 1850 - 1926
.............................................. +Sarah Jane Clark 1851 - 1925
.................................................... 6   Ada Mae Lesley 1872 -
.................................................... 6   Charles Lesley 1874 -
.................................................... 6   Mastin Leonadis Lesley 1876 -
.................................................... 6   James Theodore Lesley
.................................................... 6   Mary Daisey Lesley
.................................................... 6   Minnie Lula Lesley
.................................................... 6   Willaim Clark Lesley
.................................................... 6   James Oscar Lesley
.................................................... 6   Annie Eola Lesley
.................................................... 6   Clifford Coleman Lesley
```

2

```
................................ 6   Ruby Lillian Lesley
................................ 6   Samuel Troy Lesley
.......................... 5   James A. Lesly 1852 -
.......................... 5   William Wiley Lesly 1854 -
.......................... 5   Charles Henderson Lesly 1856 -
................................ +Caroline Rodes
................................ 6   William Theron Leslie
................................ 6   Dexter R. Leslie
................................ 6   L. Clyde Leslie
................................ 6   Charles V. Leslie
.......................... 5   Mary Moslete Lesly 1859 - 1943
...................... +Humphrey Forgy
.......................... 5   Martha Lula Lesly 1861 -
................................ +Arthur Davenport
................................ 6   Maud Davenport
................................ 6   May Davenport
................................ 6   Willie Audrey Davenport
.................. 4   James Thomas Lesly 1813 - 1897
................ +Mary Sever 1818 - 1883
.......................... 5   Madison Livingston Leslie 1844 - 1923
................ +Blanch Stephens 1848 - 1888
.................... 6   [1] James Quincy Leslie 1870 - 1944
.................... +[2] Alleen Elizabeth Shaw
.................... 7   [3] Howard L. Leslie 1900 -
.................... 7   [4] Royal D. Leslie 1903 -
.................... 7   [5] Agnes Lee Leslie 1905 -
.................... +[6] C.M.Buie
.................... 8   [7] Leslie Miller Buie
.................... 8   [8] Betty Joe Buie
.................... 8   [9] Eugene Patrick Buie
.................... 7   [10] Alyne Leslie 1907 -
.................... +[11] C.P. Dice
.................... 8   [12] Joyce Alyne Dice
.................... 8   [13] Gloria Dice
.................... 8   [14] Lera Barbara Dice
.................... 7   [15] Annie Blanche Leslie 1912 -
.................... +[16] J. S. Tuten
.................... 8   [17] Bruce Royal Tuten
.................... 8   [18] James Larry Tuten
.................... 8   [19] Glenda Tuten
.................... 8   [20] Ernie Tuten
.................... 7   [21] Nemmie Leslie 1917 -
.................... 6   [22] Mary Agnes Leslie 1871 - 1900
.................... +[23] G. W. Tedder
.................... 6   [24] John Augustus Leslie 1874 -
.................... +[25] Nora Hamilton
.................... 7   [26] Cornelia Mignon Leslie 1897 -
.................... +[27] J. Quinn Howell
.................... 8   [28] William Marvin Howell 1921 -
.................... 8   [29] Robert Eugene Howell 1925 -
.................... 8   [30] Jenne Howell 1927 -
.................... 7   [31] Fred Leslie 1902 -
.................... 7   [32] Leo Leslie 1908 -
.................... 7   [33] Hoyt Leslie 1910 -
.................... 7   [34] Cyril Leslie 1912 -
.................... 7   [35] Vesta Leslie 1913 -
.................... 7   [36] Hugo Leslie 1915 -
.................... 7   [37] Marion Leslie 1918 -
.................... 6   [38] Emma Dora Leslie 1875 - 1910
.................... +[39] Wilbur W. Grambling
.................... 7   [40] Willard Grambling 1906 -
.................... 7   [41] Myrtle Grambling
.................... 6   [42] Irene Leslie 1877 - 1938
.................... +[43] Stephen J. Duval
.................... 7   [44] Edna Josephine Duval
.................... 7   [45] Sarah Blanch Duval
.................... 7   [46] Benjamin Duval
.................... +[47] Florene Fellows
.................... 8   [48] Patricia Duval
.................... 8   [49] Barona Ann Duval
.................... 8   [50] Gwendolyn Duval
.................... 7   [51] Claude Vernon Duval
.................... +[52] Elelyn Jarvis
.................... 8   [53] Elenor Duval
.................... 8   [54] Laurie Duval
.................... 7   [55] Stephen Eustis Duval
```

3

150

```
............................................ +[56] Rachel Jarvis
............................................ 8   [57] Jackyuolyne Duval
............................................ 8   [58] Yvonne Duval
............................................ 8   [59] Larue Duval
............................................ 8   [60] Duiyne Duval
.......................................... 7   [61] Leah Duval
.......................................... 7   [62] Durward Duval
.................................. 6   [63] Blanch Indiana Leslie  1878 - 1879
.................................. 6   [64] Lawrence Madison Leslie  1880 - 1936
............................................ +[65] Winnifred . Coffee
.......................................... 7   [66] Carl M. Leslie  1911 -
.......................................... 7   [67] Courtney Leslie  1916 -
.......................................... 7   [68] Lois Leslie  1917 -
.......................................... 7   [69] Paul D. Leslie  1928 -
.................................. 6   [70] William Leroy Leslie  1882 -
.................................. 6   [71] Alpheus Moses Leslie  1883 -
............................................ +[72] Leona Gramling
.......................................... 7   [73] Loyd Leslie
.......................................... 7   [74] Clifford Leslie
.......................................... 7   [75] Madison Camillus Leslie
.......................................... 7   [76] Hazel Leslie
.......................................... 7   [77] Cecil Leslie
.................................. 6   [78] Hugh Lewis Leslie  1885 -
.................................. 6   [79] Ethel Elizabeth Leslie  1888 -
........................ *2nd Wife of Madison Livingston Leslie:
............................................ +Sarah Ponder - 1891
.......................... 6   [1] James Quincy Leslie  1870 - 1944
............................................ +[2] Alleen Elizabeth Shaw
.......................................... 7   [3] Howard L. Leslie  1900 -
.......................................... 7   [4] Royal D. Leslie  1903 -
.......................................... 7   [5] Agnes Lee Leslie  1905 -
............................................ +[6] C.M.Buie
............................................ 8   [7] Leslie Miller Buie
............................................ 8   [8] Betty Joe Buie
............................................ 8   [9] Eugene Patrick Buie
.......................................... 7   [10] Alyne Leslie  1907 -
............................................ +[11] C.P. Dice
............................................ 8   [12] Joyce Alyne Dice
............................................ 8   [13] Gloria Dice
............................................ 8   [14] Lera Barbara Dice
.......................................... 7   [15] Annie Blanche Leslie  1912 -
............................................ +[16] J. S. Tuten
............................................ 8   [17] Bruce Royal Tuten
............................................ 8   [18] James Larry Tuten
............................................ 8   [19] Glenda Tuten
............................................ 8   [20] Ernie Tuten
.......................................... 7   [21] Nemmie Leslie  1917 -
.................................. 6   [22] Mary Agnes Leslie  1871 - 1900
............................................ +[23] G. W. Tedder
.................................. 6   [24] John Augustus Leslie  1874 -
............................................ +[25] Nora Hamilton
.......................................... 7   [26] Cornelia Mignon Leslie  1897 -
............................................ +[27] J. Quinn Howell
............................................ 8   [28] William Marvin Howell  1921 -
............................................ 8   [29] Robert Eugene Howell  1925 -
............................................ 8   [30] Jenne Howell  1927 -
.......................................... 7   [31] Fred Leslie  1902 -
.......................................... 7   [32] Leo Leslie  1908 -
.......................................... 7   [33] Hoyt Leslie  1910 -
.......................................... 7   [34] Cyril Leslie  1912 -
.......................................... 7   [35] Vesta Leslie  1913 -
.......................................... 7   [36] Hugo Leslie  1915 -
.......................................... 7   [37] Marion Leslie  1918 -
.................................. 6   [38] Emma Dora Leslie  1875 - 1910
............................................ +[39] Wilbur W. Grambling
.......................................... 7   [40] Willard Grambling  1906 -
.......................................... 7   [41] Myrtle Grambling
.................................. 6   [42] Irene Leslie  1877 - 1938
............................................ +[43] Stephen J. Duval
.......................................... 7   [44] Edna Josephine Duval
.......................................... 7   [45] Sarah Blanch Duval
.......................................... 7   [46] Benjamin Duval
............................................ +[47] Florene Fellows
............................................ 8   [48] Patricia Duval
............................................ 8   [49] Barona Ann Duval
............................................ 8   [50] Gwendolyn Duval
```

4

```
..............................  7    [51] Claude Vernon Duval
..............................       +[52] Elelyn Jarvis
..............................  8     [53] Elenor Duval
..............................  8     [54] Laurie Duval
..............................  7    [55] Stephen Eustis Duval
..............................       +[56] Rachel Jarvis
..............................  8     [57] Jackyuolyne Duval
..............................  8     [58] Yvonne Duval
..............................  8     [59] Larue Duval
..............................  8     [60] Duiyne Duval
..............................  7    [61] Leah Duval
..............................  7    [62] Durward Duval
..............................  6    [63] Blanch Indiana Leslie  1878 - 1879
..............................  6    [64] Lawrence Madison Leslie  1880 - 1936
..............................       +[65] Winnifred . Coffee
..............................  7    [66] Carl M. Leslie  1911 -
..............................  7    [67] Courtney Leslie  1916 -
..............................  7    [68] Lois Leslie  1917 -
..............................  7    [69] Paul D. Leslie  1928 -
..............................  6    [70] William Leroy Leslie  1882 -
..............................  6    [71] Alpheus Moses Leslie  1883 -
..............................       +[72] Leona Gramling
..............................  7    [73] Loyd Leslie
..............................  7    [74] Clifford Leslie
..............................  7    [75] Madison Camillus Leslie
..............................  7    [76] Hazel Leslie
..............................  7    [77] Cecil Leslie
..............................  6    [78] Hugh Lewis Leslie  1885 -
..............................  6    [79] Ethel Elizabeth Leslie  1888 -
..............................  6    [80] Lillian Jane Leslie  1890 -
..............................       +[81] Walter B. Sheppard  - 1929
..............................  7    [82] Beatrice Sheppard
..............................  7    [83] Laurie C. Sheppard
..............................  7    [84] Leon L. Sheppard
..............................  7    [85] Walter B. Sheppard
..............................  *3rd Wife of Madison Livingston Leslie:
..............................  +Lizzie Clements  - 1938
..............................  6    [1] James Quincy Leslie  1870 - 1944
..............................       +[2] Alleen Elizabeth Shaw
..............................  7    [3] Howard L. Leslie  1900 -
..............................  7    [4] Royal D. Leslie  1903 -
..............................  7    [5] Agnes Lee Leslie  1905 -
..............................       +[6] C.M.Buie
..............................  8     [7] Leslie Miller Buie
..............................  8     [8] Betty Joe Buie
..............................  8     [9] Eugene Patrick Buie
..............................  7    [10] Alyne Leslie  1907 -
..............................       +[11] C.P. Dice
..............................  8     [12] Joyce Alyne Dice
..............................  8     [13] Gloria Dice
..............................  8     [14] Lera Barbara Dice
..............................  7    [15] Annie Blanche Leslie  1912 -
..............................       +[16] J. S. Tuten
..............................  8     [17] Bruce Royal Tuten
..............................  8     [18] James Larry Tuten
..............................  8     [19] Glenda Tuten
..............................  8     [20] Ernie Tuten
..............................  7    [21] Nemmie Leslie  1917 -
..............................  6    [22] Mary Agnes Leslie  1871 - 1900
..............................       +[23] G. W. Tedder
..............................  6    [24] John Augustus Leslie  1874 -
..............................       +[25] Nora Hamilton
..............................  7    [26] Cornelia Mignon Leslie  1897 -
..............................       +[27] J. Quinn Howell
..............................  8     [28] William Marvin Howell  1921 -
..............................  8     [29] Robert Eugene Howell  1925 -
..............................  8     [30] Jenne Howell  1927 -
..............................  7    [31] Fred Leslie  1902 -
..............................  7    [32] Leo Leslie  1908 -
..............................  7    [33] Hoyt Leslie  1910 -
..............................  7    [34] Cyril Leslie  1912 -
..............................  7    [35] Vesta Leslie  1913 -
..............................  7    [36] Hugo Leslie  1915 -
..............................  7    [37] Marion Leslie  1918 -
..............................  6    [38] Emma Dora Leslie  1875 - 1910
..............................       +[39] Wilbur W. Grambling
```

5

152

```
    7   [40] Willard Grambling  1906 -
    7   [41] Myrtle Grambling
    6   [42] Irene Leslie  1877 - 1938
    +[43] Stephen J. Duval
        7   [44] Edna Josephine Duval
        7   [45] Sarah Blanch Duval
        7   [46] Benjamin Duval
        +[47] Florene Fellows
            8   [48] Patricia Duval
            8   [49] Barona Ann Duval
            8   [50] Gwendolyn Duval
        7   [51] Claude Vernon Duval
        +[52] Elelyn Jarvis
            8   [53] Elenor Duval
            8   [54] Laurie Duval
        7   [55] Stephen Eustis Duval
        +[56] Rachel Jarvis
            8   [57] Jackyuolyne Duval
            8   [58] Yvonne Duval
            8   [59] Larue Duval
            8   [60] Duiyne Duval
        7   [61] Leah Duval
        7   [62] Durward Duval
    6   [63] Blanch Indiana Leslie  1878 - 1879
    6   [64] Lawrence Madison Leslie  1880 - 1936
    +[65] Winnifred . Coffee
        7   [66] Carl M. Leslie  1911 -
        7   [67] Courtney Leslie  1916 -
        7   [68] Lois Leslie  1917 -
        7   [69] Paul D. Leslie  1928 -
    6   [70] William Leroy Leslie  1882 -
    6   [71] Alpheus Moses Leslie  1883 -
    +[72] Leona Gramling
        7   [73] Loyd Leslie
        7   [74] Clifford Leslie
        7   [75] Madison Camillus Leslie
        7   [76] Hazel Leslie
        7   [77] Cecil Leslie
    6   [78] Hugh Lewis Leslie  1885 -
    6   [79] Ethel Elizabeth Leslie  1888 -
    6   [80] Lillian Jane Leslie  1890 -
    +[81] Walter B. Sheppard  - 1929
        7   [82] Beatrice Sheppard
        7   [83] Laurie C. Sheppard
        7   [84] Leon L. Sheppard
        7   [85] Walter B. Sheppard
5   Dicy Priscilla Leslie  1846 -
5   Moses Leslie  1849 - 1911
+Lettillie E. Cottingham  1850 - 1895
    6   Theodore Leslie  1871 - 1944
    +Annie Lillian Sessions  1874 -
        7   Shelton Moses Leslie  1902 -
        +Edith Harrison
            8   Shelton Eugene Leslie  1933 -
            8   Adrienne Ann Leslie  1937 -
            8   William Harrison Leslie  1942 -
    6   Arthur Leslie  1873 - 1874
    6   Andrew L. Leslie  1875 - 1937
    +Celete Cowart
        7   M.C. Leslie
        7   Mildred Leslie
        7   Leland Leslie
    6   Rosalita I. Leslie  1876 - 1877
    6   Eulalia A. Leslie  1877 -
    +W. G. Cowart
        7   James Bryant Cowart
        7   Ernest Leslie Cowart
        7   Leona Cowart
        7   Louise Cowart
        7   Andrew Cowart
        7   James Cowart
    6   Mary L. Leslie  1878 -
    6   Bertha Leslie  1879 -
    6   Louise E. Leslie  1880 - 1907
    +J. B. Cowart
        7   Rubie Cowart
```

6

```
................................ 7   Johnie Mae Cowart
..............................  6   Susan Leslie  1883 - 1883
..............................  6   John M. Leslie  1884 - 1884
..............................  6   Eliza Leslie  1885 - 1885
..............................  6   Mary Leslie  1886 -
..............................      +R. M. Allen
................................ 7   Francis Allen
................................ 7   Edgar Allen
................................ 7   Wallace Allen
..............................  6   William B. Leslie  1888 - 1889
..............................  6   Dicy P. Leslie  1889 - 1890
........................ 5   Lewis Gilliland Leslie  1851 - 1925
..........................      +Eugenia Frances Dale  1852 - 1922
..........................  6   Gertrude E. Leslie  1882 -
..............................      +William E. Tedder  - 1929
................................ 7   William E. Tedder  1906 -
................................ 7   George Lewis Tedder  1908 -
..............................      +June Mae Larin
........................... 8   George Lewis Tedder  1929 -
..........................  6   Rosalie Leslie  1883 -
..............................      +Ashley J. Nipper
................................ 7   Eugenia Nipper  1914 -
................................ 7   Lewis A, Nipper  1915 -
................................ 7   Trudie Nipper  1925 -
..........................  6   Thomas Dale Leslie  1885 -
..............................      +Lydia Mctear
..........................  6   Lewis Eugene Leslie  1890 -
..............................      +Bessie Henderson
................................ 7   Hillouise Leslie  1914 -
..............................      +Joe Bevin
........................... 8   Richard James Bevin  1935 -
................................ 7   Dale M. Leslie  1917 -
..........................  6   Tolliver M. Leslie  1894 - 1928
..............................      +Inez V. Bullard  - 1933
................................ 7   Laura Frances Leslie  1924 -
................................ 7   Jacqueline V. Leslie  1925 -
................................ 7   Tolliver Madison Leslie  1929 -
........................ 5   Charles Leslie  1854 -
........................ 5   William Sever Leslie  1855 - 1928
..........................      +Fannie Edwards  - 1893
..........................  6   Florrie Aline Leslie  1892 -
..............................      +Grover C. Allmon
................................ 7   James Ganey Allmon  1916 -
................................ 7   Hallie Poston Allmon  1919 -
................................ 7   Ruth Brinson Allmon  1923 -
..........................      *2nd Wife of William Sever Leslie:
..........................      +Mollie Edwards  - 1898
..........................  6   Ruth Beatrice Leslie  1896 -
..........................  6   Sidney Holiday Leslie  1898 -
..............................      +Mary Rebecca Long  1903 -
................................ 7   William Thomas Leslie  1930 -
................................ 7   Robert Eugene Leslie  1931 -
................................ 7   Mary Florence Leslie  1934 -
........................ 5   Mary Indiana Leslie  1856 - 1935
..........................      +William Franklin Howard  1849 - 1933
..........................  6   Mary Sever Howard  1876 - 1944
..............................      +William C. Caulk
................................ 7   Charles Colon Caulk  1896 -
..............................      +Marion Morse  - 1930
................................ 7   Mary Lee Caulk  1914 -
..........................  6   Stella Mabel Howard  1878 - 1880
..........................  6   Willie Elizabeth Howard  1881 -
..............................      +Edward B. Weathers
................................ 7   Mabel Weathers  1923 -
..............................      +Thomas L. Clyath
................................ 7   William Walter Weathers  1924 -
..........................  6   Mattie Mabel Howard  1884 -
..............................      +Albert Clinton McMullen
................................ 7   Jamnes Howard McMullen  1905 -
................................ 7   William Eugene McMullen  1907 -
..........................  6   Ola Eugenia Howard  1887 -
..............................      +John McKnight
..........................  6   George Leslie Howard  1890 -
..............................      +Beulah Jordan
................................ 7   Nina Gladys Howard  1916 -
..............................      +Phillip D. McRae
```

7

```
.................................. 7  Lottie Ruth Howard  1918 -
.................................. +George James Hornaday
.................................. 7  Edna Mae Howard  1922 -
.................................. 6  Maude Madison Howard  1893 -
.................................. +Robert Lee Walker
.................................. 7  Randall Howard Walker  1912 - 1933
.................................. 7  Maude Evelyn Walker  1914 -
.................................. 7  Doris Marie Walker  1919 -
.................................. +Alfred Rankin Cox, Jr.
.................................. 8  Alfred Rankin Cox III  1942 -
.................................. 7  Eugene Loyd Walker  1925 -
.................................. 7  William Leslie Walker  1926 -
.................................. 6  Ruby Lielillie Howard  1896 -
.................................. +Otis Carlos Sistrunk
.................................. 7  Walter Everett Sistrunk  1920 -
.................................. +Marion Smith
.................................. 7  Joanna Sistrunk  1923 -
.................................. 7  Maude Eugenia Sistrunk  1925 -
.................................. 7  Minor Montholan Sistrunk  1927 -
.................................. 6  Clyde Maurice Howard  1899 -
.................................. +Pauline Taylor
.................................. 4  Frances A Lesly  1809 - 1889
.................................. +Andrew Jackson Sims  - 1847
.................................. 5  Mary Ann Josephine Sims  1835 - 1875
.................................. 5  Louisa Sims  1837 - 1848
.................................. 5  Frances Pamah Sims  1838 - 1838
.................................. 5  Indianna Sims  1839 - 1928
.................................. 5  John Andrew Jackson Sims  1841 -
.................................. 5  Jefferson J. Sims  1845 -
.................................. 4  Joseph Lesly  1819 -
.................................. 4  Mary Lesly  1819 -
.................................. 4  Mary E. Lesly  1821 - 1846
.................................. 4  John Lesly  1823 -
.................................. 3  Jane Lesly  1786 - 1807
.................................. 3  Robert Hall Lesly  1787 - 1847
.................................. +Elizabeth Watt  1786 - 1830
.................................. 4  Jane Ann Lesly  1810 - 1898
.................................. +John Glenn Fraser  - 1840
.................................. 4  James Lewis Lesly  1812 - 1891
.................................. +Eliza Wilson  - 1837
.................................. 5  Eliza Lulah Lesly  1837 -
.................................. *2nd Wife of James Lewis Lesly:
.................................. +Charlotte Montague Watkins  1819 - 1875
.................................. 5  Cornelia Ellen Lesly  1846 - 1911
.................................. 5  Mary Lavinia Lesly  1847 - 1914
.................................. 5  Emma Eugenia Lesly  1849 - 1908
.................................. 5  Annie Laurie Lesly  1857 - 1862
.................................. 5  Lewis Watkins Lesly  1863 -
.................................. 4  Samuel Lesly  1815 -
.................................. 4  William Andrew Lesly  1817 - 1877
.................................. +Virginia White
.................................. 4  John Watt Lesly  1819 - 1892
.................................. +Louisa Jane McWhorter  1842 - 1919
.................................. 5  Anna Louise Lesly  1867 - 1897
.................................. 5  William David Lesly  1868 - 1944
.................................. +Jennie Daisy Verner
.................................. 6  William Henry Lesly  1895 -
.................................. 6  Jennie Marie Lesly  1897 -
.................................. 6  Glenn Verner Lesly  1902 -
.................................. 6  Fred Scott Lesly  1904 -
.................................. 5  John Watt Lesly  1869 - 1923
.................................. +Gussie Duke
.................................. 6  Elisa May Lesly  1921 -
.................................. 6  Mary Louise Lesly  1923 -
.................................. 5  Thomas Lesly  1872 - 1892
.................................. 5  Marquerita Lesly  1876 -
.................................. +Handy Eugene Fant
.................................. 6  Louise Lesley Fant  1902 -
.................................. 6  Handy Bruce Fant  1903 -
.................................. 6  Mary Eugenia Fant  1906 -
.................................. 6  Kyle Lesley Fant  1908 -
.................................. 6  William Carlisle Fant  1910 -
.................................. 6  Glenn Ernest Fant  1912 -
.................................. 5  Glenn Fraser Lesley  1879 - Unknown
.................................. +Emily Beckley Wall
.................................. 6  Hubert Lesley  1909 -
```

8

```
............................................ +Kathryn Williams
...................................... 7   Robert Glenn Lesley  1940 -
...................................... 7   James Richard Lesley  1940 -
.................................. 7   Donald Williams Lesley  1944 -
........................... 5   James Kyle Lesley  1882 - 1944
........................... +Myrtle Lucretia Steele
.................................. 6   Harriet Louise Lesley  1909 -
.................................. 6   Myrtle Luretia Lesley  1910 -
.................................. 6   Mary Elizabeth Lesley  1913 -
.................................. 6   Ruth Caroline Lesley  1916 -
.................................. 6   Grace Lenora Lesley  1920 -
.................................. 6   James Robert Lesley  1923 -
.................................. 6   Lillian Madge Lesley  1926 -
.................................. 6   Dorothy Jane Lesley  1930 -
..................... 4   Robert L. Lesly  1822 -
..................... 4   Cornelia Lesly  1824 -
..................... 4   Thomas Harris Lesly  1828 - 1862
.............. 3   Elizabeth  1789 - 1807
.............. 3   Ann  1791 - 1863
.................. +Samuel Jack
.............. 3   William Lesly  1793 - 1867
................. +Martha Emily White  1811 - 1842
...................... 4   Anna Louisa Lesly  1828 - 1859
........................ +Col. Jesse Ward Norris
............................ 5   Martha (Mattie)Lesley Norris  1854 - 1926
............................ +John W. Thomson  1850 - 1924
.................................... 6   Ward Norris Thomson  1876 - 1918
.................................... +Corrie Belle Godbold  1880 - 1941
......................................... 7   John White Thomson  1901 -
......................................... +Elvira Marella Redlund
............................................... 8   John Redlund Thomson  1932 -
............................................... 8   Francis Marion Thomson  1936 -
.......................................... 7   Sarah Vance Thomson  1905 -
.......................................... +A. Beaty Jackson
.......................................... 7   Ward Norris Thomson  1907 -
.................................... 6   Mary Thomson  1878 -
.................................... 6   James Thomson  1880 -
.................................... 6   Louisa Lesly Thomson  1882 -
............................ 5   Lucy Riah (Lulie) Norris  1857 - 1915
............................ +William David Simpson  1852 - 1915
.................................... 6   Bessie Simpson  1881 -
.................................... +Will Chester Plant  1879 - 1916
......................................... 7   Elsie Plant  1916 -
.................................... 6   Leslie Norris Simpson  1883 -
.................................... +Jonnie Hancock
.................................... 6   William David Simpson  1886 -
.................................... +Janie Hyde Harris  1900 -
......................................... 7   Jane Hunter Simpson  1921 -
......................................... 7   Adele Hyde Simpson  1927 -
......................................... 7   Elizabeth Norris Simpson  1927 -
.................................... 6   Joseph Bratton Simpson  1886 -
.................................... +Pearle Bolt
......................................... 7   Lillian Norris Simpson  1924 -
.................................... 6   Jesse Ward Simpson  1892 -
.................................... +Sata Spearman
......................................... 7   Jesse Ward Simpson  1919 -
......................................... +Martha Winn
............................ 5   Mary Norris
..................... 4   Augustus Lesly  1830 - 1830
..................... 4   Virginia Elizabeth Lesly  1832 - 1903
..................... +James Archibald Montgomery  1832 - 1910
.......................... 5   William Archibald Montgomery  1857 - 1902
.......................... 5   Mary Louise Montgomery  1862 - 1862
.......................... 5   Elvira Virginia Montgomery  1866 - 1867
.......................... 5   Ella Lewis Montgomery  1868 - 1934
.......................... +John Calhoun Black
.......................... 5   Ernest Lesley Montgomery  1869 -
.......................... +Cora Sale McLees
................................ 6   James Robert Montgomery  1904 -
................................ +Sarah Ethlyn Black
..................................... 7   Robert Laurens Montgomery  1926 -
..................................... 7   Charles Montgomery  1932 -
..................................... 7   Marion Montgomery  1935 -
................................ 6   Virginia Elvira Montgomery  1909 -
................................ +Paul McElrath
..................................... 7   Carolyn McElrath  1936 -
```

9

156

```
.........................................  7   Barbara McElrath  1938 -
.........................................  7   Ann Margaret McElrath  1942 -
.........................................  6   Ernest Willie Montgomery  1910 -
.........................................  +Mary Craton Pruitt
.........................................  7   Doris Crayton Montgomery  1933 -
.........................................  7   Mary Ernestine Montgomery  1938 -
.........................................  7   Nany Eleanor Montgomery  1942 -
.........................................  6   Anna Lewis Montgomery  1912 -
.........................................  +Marvin Ashley
.........................................  7   Marvin Ann Ashley  1936 -
.........................................  6   Henry Davis Montgomery  1915 -
.........................................  +Elizabeth Williamson
.........................................  6   Frank Brown Montgomery  1920 -
.........................................  +Mattie Loskoskie
.........................................  7   James Frank Montgomery  1943 -
.........................................  6   Homer Sale Montgomery  1924 -
.........................................  5   May Ola Montgomery  1871 -
.........................................  5   Alvin David Montgomery  1874 -
.........................................  4  Alpheus Ezekiel Lesly  1834 - 1905
.........................................  +Virginia Miller  1839 - 1892
.........................................  5   William Edwin Leslie  1868 - 1939
.........................................  +Annie Donnald Henry  1873 - 1946
.........................................  6   William Edwin Leslie, Jr.  1895 - 1965
.........................................  +Glendel Bowen  1899 - 1982
.........................................  7   William Leslie III  1923 - 1996
.........................................  8   william Belmont Leslie
.........................................  7   Marcelene Leslie  1929 -
.........................................  +William Chambers Myers  1926 -
.........................................  8   William (Dub)Chambers Myers, Jr.  1951 -
.........................................  +Shirley Kay Bodie
.........................................  9   William Belmont Myers
.........................................  9   Kate Myers
.........................................  9   Nick Myers
.........................................  *2nd Wife of William (Dub)Chambers Myers, Jr.:
.........................................  +Laura Belmont
.........................................  9   William Belmont Myers  1986 -
.........................................  8   Marcelene Leslie Myers  1953 -
.........................................  8   Leisa Weston Myers  1957 -
.........................................  8   Melissa Westbury Myers  1960 -
.........................................  8   Laurie Leslie Myers  1964 -
.........................................  6   Frank Henry Leslie  1896 - 1985
.........................................  +Carmin Ericson
.........................................  6   Alpheus Ezekiel Leslie  1898 - 1986
.........................................  +Lucy Kathryne Sturdivant  1898 - 1986
.........................................  7   Robert Edward Leslie  1925 - 2007
.........................................  +Jane Moore  1929 -
.........................................  8   Martha Ann Leslie  1953 -
.........................................  +Michael Wayne Alley  1950 -
.........................................  9   Edward Warren Alley
.........................................  9   Jane Leslie Alley  1982 -
.........................................  7   Alpheus Ezekiel Leslie, Jr.  1927 -
.........................................  +Kathryne Greer  1929 - 1990
.........................................  *2nd Wife of Alpheus Ezekiel Leslie, Jr.:
.........................................  +Lafern Jones
.........................................  7   Donald William Leslie  1931 -
.........................................  +Marian Belle Henderson  1934 -
.........................................  8   Susan Kaye Leslie  1957 -
.........................................  +Michael Roy Vaughn
.........................................  9   Allison Leslie Vaughn  1987 -
.........................................  9   Audrey Katherine Vaughn  1993 -
.........................................  8   Donald William Leslie, Jr.  1959 - 1973
.........................................  8   Henry Miller Leslie  1961 - 2011
.........................................  +Pamela Davis
.........................................  *2nd Wife of Henry Miller Leslie:
.........................................  +Mary Allen
.........................................  7   Mary Sturdivant Leslie  1934 -
.........................................  +James Haddon Williams  1932 -
.........................................  8   Mary Jeanne Williams  1959 -
.........................................  +Bruce Empey
.........................................  9   Breanne Empey
.........................................  10  Graham Empey
.........................................  9   Taylor Empey
.........................................  8   Leslie Lynne Williams  1962 -
.........................................  +Osman A. Hicklin III (Bud)
.........................................  9   James A. Hicklin
.........................................  9   Evan Hicklin
```

10
157

```
.................................................... 8   Laura Elizabeth Williams  1965 -
.................................................... 8   Lucy Jana Williams  1971 -
....................................................     +Tim Ramsey
....................................................         9   Jayce Ramsey  1994 -
.................................................... *2nd Husband of Lucy Jana Williams:
....................................................     +Ed Nelson
....................................................         9   Riley Nelson  1996 -
....................................................         9   Kaitlyn Nelson  2003 -
.................................... 6   Albert Henry Leslie  1898 - 1978
....................................    +Margaret Sydelle Graves  1901 - 1991
........................................ 7   Jean Ellen Leslie  1924 - 1994
........................................    +Harold Hutson Winters  1921 - 2004
........................................ 8   Harold Hutson Winters, Jr.  1952 -
........................................    +Susan Ford Randolph  1955 - 2000
........................................         9   Alan Michael Winters  1985 -
.................................... 8   Leslie Ann Winters  1955 -
....................................    +Robert Gerald Everitt  1953 -
....................................         9   Brian Ross Everitt  1985 -
....................................         9   Kelly Jean Everitt  1990 -
.............................. 7   Margaret Sydelle Leslie  1926 - 2008
..............................    +Frank Albert Meyer  1924 - 2008
..............................         8   Martin Leslie Meyer  1956 -
..............................         8   Jeffrey Frederick Meyer  1958 - 1979
..............................         8   Wendy Elezabeth Meyer  1962 -
..........................             +Joel Goodwin
..............................             9   Andrew Heath Goodwin  1992 -
..............................             9   Isabelle Ellen Goodwin  1995 -
.............................. 7   Ann Henry Leslie  1932 -
..............................    +George Johnson Maust,Jr  1930 - 2006
..............................         8   Kimbal Ann Maust  1957 -
..............................             +William Empson  1946 -
..............................             9   Justin R. Empson  1981 -
..............................                 +Amber
..............................             9   Jesse William Empson  1984 -
..............................         8   Gregory Allen Maust  1959 - 2005
..............................             +Catherine Diane Morrison
..............................         8   Robert Johnson Maust  1961 -
..............................             +Johanna Cecelia Thoren  1973 -
..............................             9   Jacob Johnson Maust  1998 -
..............................             9   Noah George Maust  2000 -
..............................             9   Adam Olaf Maust  2000 -
..............................             9   Emma Cecelia Maust  2005 -
.................................... 6   David Hill Leslie  1900 - 1971
....................................    +Thelma Hagen
....................................         7   Niholas Miller Leslie  1936 - 1987
....................................         7   Harper D. Leslie  1937 - 1968
....................................         7   Gene Awtrey Leslie  1940 - 1967
....................................         7   William Edwin Leslie  1943 -
....................................         7   Jerry D. Leslie  1946 - 1947
.................................... 6   Virginia Miller Leslie  1902 -
.................................... 6   John Donnald Leslie  1904 - 1951
....................................    +Georgia Philbert  1917 - 2006
....................................         7   Donnald Philbert Leslie  1939 -
....................................             +Elizabeth
....................................         7   Margaret Ann Leslie (Peggy)  1940 -
....................................             +George Amos Pierce, Jr.
....................................             8   Leslie Ann Pierce  1965 -
....................................             8   Patricia Ann Pierce  1967 -
....................................             8   Virginia Ann Pierce  1971 -
....................................    *2nd Husband of Margaret Ann Leslie (Peggy):
....................................        +Clarence Agustus(Gus) Jeter III  1940 -
.................................... 6   Sarah Ellen Leslie  1906 -
....................................    +Rudolph S.A. Thunberg
....................................         7   Ann Leslie Thunberg  1934 -
....................................             +Wayne Yelverton  1931 -
....................................         7   Rudolph Thunberg  1938 -
....................................             +Debrorah Ann Jamroz  1953 -
....................................             8   Ellen Leslie Thunberg  1986 -
.................................... 6   Robert Hall Leslie  1909 - 1986
....................................    +Dorothy Eloise Nickles  1912 - 2003
....................................         7   Robert Hall Leslie, Jr.(Bobby)  1938 -
....................................             +Martha Carolayn Bell  1942 -
....................................             8   Robert Ted Leslie (Ted)  1963 -
....................................                 +Lydia Mac Horton  1966 -
....................................                 9   Lauren Nicole Leslie  1996 -
....................................                 9   Robert Nieckles Leslie  1998 -
```

11

158

```
..........................................................  9  Mitchell Benton Leslie  2000 -
.......................................................  8  Debra Carol Leslie  1966 -
....................................................  +Rodney Brooks Grizzle  1966 -
...........................................................  9  Parker Brooks Grizzle  1996 -
...............................................................  9  Logan Carter Grizzle  1998 -
...........................................  8  Denis Scott Leslie  1968 -
.....................................................  +Nova Marie Leslie  1970 -
..............................................................  9  Samuel Scott Leslie  2001 -
...............................................................  9  Mary Elizabeth Leslie  2004 -
..............................................  7  Charles Edward Leslie  1940 -
....................................................  +Christine Sccott Goodenough  1944 -
.........................................  8  Tina Marie Leslie (Tina)  1962 -
.........................................................  +Batchler
..............................................................  9  Christina Marie Batchler  1996 -
.........................................  8  Michael Charles Leslie (Mike)  1965 -
....................................................  +Laura Kelling  1968 -
...............................................................  9  Carolyn Baker Leslie (Baker)  1998 -
..............................................................  9  Catherine Hope Leslie (Hope)  2000 -
.......................................  *2nd Wife of Charles Edward Leslie:
...............................................  +Earline Lisk  1942 -
..............................  7  William Benton Leslie (Benton)  1944 - 1994
....................................................  +Fayer Hammond
..............................  7  Mary Louise Leslie (Louise)  1946 -
....................................................  +Benny Richard Davis  1944 -
.........................................  8  Leslie Lynn Davis  1969 -
....................................................  +George L. Johnson III (Jay)  1969 -
..............................................................  9  George Franklin Johnson  1998 -
..............................................................  9  Landyn Nicole Johnson  2002 -
..............................................................  9  Abby Grace Johnson  2003 -
.........................................  8  Karen Suzanne Davis  1977 -
....................................................  +Chad Joseph Heery  1974 -
..............................................................  9  Madison Louise Heery  2006 -
..............................  6  Mac Henry Leslie  1911 - 1979
....................................................  +Francis Lawton Botts
..............................  6  James Lewis Leslie  1913 -
....................................................  +Martha Olivia Wilson  1919 -
..............................  7  James Lewis Leslie (Jimmy)  1942 -
....................................................  +Gertrude Denise Fox  1942 -
.........................................  8  Jennifer Denise Leslie  1970 -
..............................  7  Marie Ann Leslie (Ann)  1945 -
....................................................  +Franklin Eugene Pursrley  1945 -
.........................................  8  Carol Lynn Pursrley  1970 -
....................................................  +Gary Goss  1967 -
..............................................................  9  Grayson Holloway Goss  2000 -
..............................................................  9  Caroline Olivia Goss  2001 -
.........................................  8  Leigh Ann Pursrley  1973 -
....................................................  +Igor Zikus  1979 -
..............................  7  Henry Stephen Leslie (Steve)  1950 -
....................................................  +Connie Price  1952 -
.........................................  8  Scott Stephen Leslie  1974 -
....................................................  +Kimberly Ann Schultz  1974 -
.........................................  8  Alison Michele Leslie  1977 -
....................................................  +Shawn Lewis Hanna  1975 -
..............................................................  9  Catherine Riggins Hanna  2012 -
.........................................  8  Amanda Brooke Leslie  1980 -
....................................................  +Daniel Patrick Harris  1981 -
.........................................  8  Todd Michael Leslie  1984 -
.......................................  *2nd Wife of Henry Stephen Leslie (Steve):
...............................................  +Thelma Nabors George  1959 -
..............................  6  Nicholas Miller Leslie  1915 - 1989
....................................................  +Mary Edwards  1918 - 1975
..............................  7  Nicholas Miller Leslie, Jr.  1953 -
....................................................  +Pamela Sue North  1953 -
.........................................  8  Mary Elizabeth Leslie  1983 -
.........................................  8  Andrew North Leslie  1986 -
..............................  7  Robin Anne Leslie  1955 -
....................................................  +W. Thomas Copeland
.........................................  8  Casey Elizabeth Copeland  1983 -
....................................................  +David Bradford  1973 -
..............................................................  9  Ranelaugh Rosemary Bradford
.......................................  *2nd Husband of Robin Anne Leslie:
...............................................  +Everett Malcolm
..............................  6  Annie Donnald Leslie  1918 - 2004
....................................................  +Uriah Franklin Corkrum
..............................  7  Virginia Ann Corkrum  1948 -
....................................................  +Roger Hope  1941 -
```

12

```
..........................................................  8   Steven Uriah Hope 1975 -
..........................................................  8   Nathaniel Wallace Hope 1977 -
..........................................................  8   Natalie Ann Hope 1979 -
..........................................................  8   Maribeth Nina Hope 1980 -
..........................................................  ·8   Alexander William Hope 1982 -
..........................................................  8   Sarah Marie Hope 1985 -
..........................................................  8   John David Hope 1987 -
..........................................................  7  Uriah Franklin Corkrum, Jr. 1949 -
..........................................................  7  Marion Barlow Corkrum 1953 -
..........................................  6
..........................................  6
..........................................  6
..........................  4   John Joseph Lesly 1838 -
..................  3   Thomas 1795 - 1829
..................  3   David 1797 - 1854
......................  +Louisa Kyle
..................  3   Ezekiel 1799 - 1809
........  *2nd Wife of William Lesly:
..............  +Miss. Lesly Unknown - Unknown
..................  3   Samuel Watt 1803 - 1877
........  2   Margaret Lesslie 1757 -
........  2   Thomas Lesslie 1760 - 1839
..............  +Mary Harris - 1843
..................  3   Jane M. Lesly 1785 -
..................  3   William Harris Lesly 1786 -
..................  3   John Lesly 1787 -
..................  3   Margaret W. Lesly 1790 -
......................  +Preston Starrett
..................  3   James Lesly 1792 -
......................  +AnnMcClellan Edington
..................  3   Samuel Lesly 1795 -
......................  +Margaret Hamilton
..................  3   Mary Ann Lesly 1798 -
..................  3   Andrew Lesly 1800 -
..................  3   Thomas Lesly 1805 - 1881
......................  +Nancy Shadden 1804 - 1857
..........................  4   [86] Alexander Leslie 1838 - 1838
..........................  4   [87] William Leslie 1839 - 1852
..........................  +[88] Martha King
..................  5   [89] King Leslie 1862 -
..........................  5   [90] Leonard Jason Leslie 1865 - 1947
..........................  +[91] Margaret Bowland 1865 - 1947
..........................  6   [92] William Phillip Leslie 1887 - 1950
..........................  +[93] Edna Rachel Bradshaw 1896 - 1987
..........................  6   [94] Fannie Leslie 1890 - 1961
..........................  +[95] William Abraham Sudderth 1888 - 1925
..........................  6   [96] Henry Franklin Leslie 1893 - 1984
..........................  +[97] Loy Scarbrough 1897 - 1983
..........................  6   [98] Esther May Leslie 1894 - 1925
..........................  +[99] Earl (Chub) Smith 1898 - 1975
..........................  6   [100] Homer Gilbert Leslie 1896 - 1937
..........................  +[101] Bessie Pence 1897 -
..........................  6   [102] George L. Leslie 1900 - 1976
..........................  +[103] Reva Bradshaw - 1973
..........................  6   [104] Hubert B. Leslie 1903 - 1982
..........................  +[105] Marion Maxwell
..................  4   [106] Mary Leslie 1842 - 1902
..........................  +[107] Andrew Shadden
..................  4   [108] James Wiley Leslie 1843 - 1913
..........................  +[109] Nancy Elizabeth Lee 1853 - 1934
..................  5   [110] Thomas Edward Leslie 1872 - 1942
..........................  +[111] Buena Curd 1877 - 1971
..................  5   [112] Ida Sue Leslie 1875 -
..........................  +[113] Pryor Watson - 1928
..................  5   [114] Esther Macon Leslie 1877 -
..........................  +[115] Nathaniel J. Watson
..................  5   [116] Ulysess Grant Leslie 1880 - 1946
..........................  +[117] Betty Brokehill 1889 - 1965
..................  5   [118] Edith Elizabeth Leslie 1883 - 1965
..........................  +[119] Verlin O. Fleenor
..................  5   [120] Lee Wiley Leslie 1885 - 1955
..........................  +[121] Caroline F. Blackman 1883 - 1936
..................  5   [122] Priscella Sue Leslie 1887 - 1973
..........................  +[123] Eugene Moser
..................  5   [124] George Washington Leslie 1891 - 1971
..........................  +[125] Annie Lenora Schaffer 1896 -
```

13

```
.................... 4  [126] Thomas Leslie 1845 - 1902
....................    +[127] Susan L. Lee
.................... 4  [128] John (Jack) Leslie 1848 - 1929
....................    +[129] Lutitia Payne
.................... 4  [86] Alexander Leslie 1838 - 1838
.................... 4  [87] William Leslie 1839 - 1852
....................    +[88] Martha King
...................... 5  [89] King Leslie 1862 -
...................... 5  [90] Leonard Jason Leslie 1865 - 1947
......................    +[91] Margaret Bowland 1865 - 1947
........................ 6  [92] William Phillip Leslie 1887 - 1950
........................    +[93] Edna Rachel Bradshaw 1896 - 1987
........................ 6  [94] Fannie Leslie 1890 - 1961
........................    +[95] William Abraham Sudderth 1888 - 1925
........................ 6  [96] Henry Franklin Leslie 1893 - 1984
........................    +[97] Loy Scarbrough 1897 - 1983
........................ 6  [98] Esther May Leslie 1894 - 1925
........................    +[99] Earl (Chub) Smith 1898 - 1975
........................ 6  [100] Homer Gilbert Leslie 1896 - 1937
........................    +[101] Bessie Pence 1897 -
........................ 6  [102] George L. Leslie 1900 - 1976
........................    +[103] Reva Bradshaw - 1973
........................ 6  [104] Hubert B. Leslie 1903 - 1982
........................    +[105] Marion Maxwell
.................... 4  [106] Mary Leslie 1842 - 1902
....................    +[107] Andrew Shadden
.................... 4  [108] James Wiley Leslie 1843 - 1913
....................    +[109] Nancy Elizabeth Lee 1853 - 1934
...................... 5  [110] Thomas Edward Leslie 1872 - 1942
......................    +[111] Buena Curd 1877 - 1971
...................... 5  [112] Ida Sue Leslie 1875 -
......................    +[113] Pryor Watson - 1928
...................... 5  [114] Esther Macon Leslie 1877 -
......................    +[115] Nathaniel J. Watson
...................... 5  [116] Ulysess Grant Leslie 1880 - 1946
......................    +[117] Betty Brokehill 1889 - 1965
...................... 5  [118] Edith Elizabeth Leslie 1883 - 1965
......................    +[119] Verlin O. Fleenor
...................... 5  [120] Lee Wiley Leslie 1885 - 1955
......................    +[121] Caroline F. Blackman 1883 - 1936
...................... 5  [122] Priscella Sue Leslie 1887 - 1973
......................    +[123] Eugene Moser
...................... 5  [124] George Washington Leslie 1891 - 1971
......................    +[125] Annie Lenora Schaffer 1896 -
.................... 4  [126] Thomas Leslie 1845 - 1902
....................    +[127] Susan L. Lee
.................... 4  [128] John (Jack) Leslie 1848 - 1929
....................    +[129] Lutitia Payne
.................... 4  Samuel Leslie 1864 - 1866
.................... 4  [130] Jane Ann Leslie 1866 - 1899
....................    +[131] William B. McClellan
.................... 4  [132] Andrew Leslie 1868 - 1890
..................    *2nd Wife of Thomas Lesly:
....................    +Martha Cass
.................... 4  Samuel Leslie 1864 - 1866
.................... 4  [130] Jane Ann Leslie 1866 - 1899
....................    +[131] William B. McClellan
.................... 4  [132] Andrew Leslie 1868 - 1890
........ 2  Jane Lesslie 1763 -
```

14

BIBLIOGRAPHY

Ware, Dr. Lowery, **Old Abbeville, Scenes of the Past of a Town Where Old Time Things Are Not Forgotten**. SCMAR, Columbia, South Carolina 1992

Klieforth, Alexander Leslie, Munro, Robert John, **The Scottish Invention of America**. University Press of America, Inc., Lanham, Maryland

Klieforth, Alexander Leslie, **Grip Fast: The Leslies In History**. Phillimore & Co. LTD. Shopwyke Manor Barn, Chichester, Sussex

The Journal Of Scotch-Irish Studies, Center For Scotch-Irish Studies. Published by Harold R. Aleander, Glenolden, Pennsylvania

Edgar, Walter B., **South Carolina, A History**, University Of South Carolina Press, Columbia, South Carolina

Fischer, David Hackett, **Albions Seed, Four British Folkways in America**, Oxford University Press, New York, Oxford 1989

Bailyn, Bernard, **Voyages to the West, A Passage in the Peopling of America on the Eve of the Revolution**, Vintage Books, A Division of Random House, New York, 1988

Bailyn, Bernard, **The Peopling of North America, An Introduction**, Vintage Books, A Division of Random House, New York, 1988

Webb, James, **Born Fighting, How the Scots-Irish Shaped America**, Broadway Books, New York, 2004

Bolton, Charles Knowles, **Scotch Irish Pioneers, In Ulster and America**, Heritage Books, Inc, Bowie, Maryland 1989

Bardon, Jonathon, **A History of Ulster, The Blackstaff Press Limited**, 3 Galway Park, Dundonald, Belfast, Northern Ireland 1992

Coit, Margaret L., **John C. Calhoun, American Portrait**

Leyburn, James G., **The Scotch-Irish, A Social History**, The University of North Carolina Press 1962

Lathan, Rev. Robert, D.D., **History of South Carolina**

Leslie, Colonel Charles K.H. of Balquhain, **Historical Records of the Family of Leslie from 1067 to 1868-9**, Edmonston and Douglas, 1869

Logan, John, **History of Upper Carolina**

Macaulay, Lord Thomas Babbington, **A History of England**

Mackie, J.D., **A History of Scotland**

Ferguson, Lester, **Abbeville County History**

Stevenson, Mrs. Pearl M., **Keeping the Faith, A History of Upper Long Cane Presbyterian Church**